Reader's Digest
Wild**Britain**

GARDEN
BIRDS

PUBLISHED BY
THE READER'S DIGEST ASSOCIATION LIMITED
LONDON ▪ NEW YORK ▪ SYDNEY ▪ MONTREAL

D0101531

CONTENTS

BIRDS 22

BIRD WATCHING AND BEHAVIOUR 218

HOW TO USE THIS BOOK

THE BIRDS DESCRIBED in this book are arranged in their family groups, starting with the more primitive families and ending with the most advanced species – the passerines, or perching birds. Becoming familiar with the family groups will narrow the search to decide which species you have seen. In 'How birds are grouped' (pages 14-21), all the families of birds likely to be seen in gardens and parks are listed and described, and one or more birds from each group are illustrated. These are the first pages to turn to when you spot an unfamiliar bird. Check through the descriptions and illustrations, to establish in which group the bird belongs. Then turn to the relevant pages in the main part of the book to complete the identification.

For beginners to birdwatching, 'How to identify garden birds' (pages 8-13) explains techniques of bird identification that you can use when birdwatching locally. By looking at these pages you can train your eye to spot the essential characteristics of different species.

Sometimes there are marked differences between the plumages of males and females of the same species, or between their winter and summer or adult and juvenile plumages. These are illustrated on the relevant species pages.

How to read the maps

Distribution maps in the main part of the book show when and where you are most likely to see each species. The time of year when you see a bird, or the part of the British Isles where you see it, can be useful clues to its identity.

 PURPLE *shows the usual breeding range of summer visitors*

GREEN *shows the areas where a resident species breeds and remains all year round*

BLUE *shows the areas where a species is found in winter*

GREY *indicates where passage migrants occur*

The winter range of birds and that of passage migrants are less precise than the breeding range of resident birds or summer visitors because they depend on factors such as the severity of the weather. All birds, particularly passage migrants, sometimes appear outside their usual range.

How birds are classified

The modern system of classification groups birds according to their evolutionary relationship with one another, and gives each of them a set of scientific names.

SPECIES The basic unit of the modern system is the species, an interbreeding group of individuals.

GENUS The next, larger division is the genus, a group of closely related species of birds, usually showing obvious similarities. The black-headed gull, for instance, is one of many species that belong to the main gull genus, *Larus* (the name is a Latinised version of the Greek word meaning a rapacious seabird, probably a gull). A bird's scientific name always states the genus first, then the species. The black-headed gull is called *Larus ridibundus* – translated literally, the name means 'Gull, laughing'. Genus and species names are always written in italics, but families, orders and other groups are not.

FAMILIES When one genus closely resembles another, they are grouped together to make a family. Gulls are similar in many ways to terns, and both belong to the family Laridae, named after the Greek word for a gull. Their closest relatives are the terns in the family Sternidae. All bird families are grouped into about 30 different orders. The family of gulls and terns belong, together with a great variety of other sea and shore birds, in a number of different families of the order Charadriiformes, named after the Greek for 'plover'.

CLASS All the orders together make up the zoological class *Aves* – 'Birds'.

How to identify garden birds

TAKE A LOOK AT the kind of bird you can see in your garden: is it on a feeder or a bird table, feeding on the ground beneath or on the lawn, in the flowerbed or in a tree? Is it as tiny as a sparrow or as big as a blackbird or a pigeon?

Tiny, acrobatic titmice come to feeders – perhaps blue-green-and-yellow ones (blue and great tits) or dull brown and black ones (coal, marsh and willow tits). Watch out for the black-crowned blackcap, which comes to some bird tables in winter. Look at the different way it moves – this is a warbler, with little of the agility of

the stumpy-bodied, short-legged, strong-footed tits.

Thrushes form a group of medium-small birds – blackbird, song and mistle thrushes, redwing and fieldfare – all sharing a stocky body, longish tail, stout beak, thick legs and a steady, hop-cum-walk on the ground. The starling is similar but has a short tail and runs or waddles in quick bursts, although its variety of plumages, from the dull brown of young ones to the shiny, iridescence of summer birds and

Blackbird
page 136

Blackcap
page 142

Wood pigeon
page 70

Magpie
page 180

Coal tit
page 168

Blue tit
page 164

heavy white spots of autumn and winter ones, can cause identification problems.

Some birds are unmistakable, like the robin. But even the bright, freshly feathered robin of winter and early spring is a pale shadow of its old self by late summer. Young robins are simply brown and spotted at first, but they have the typical cocky robin shape. You will soon be able to tell a robin, or a blackbird or starling, by their 'personality' – shape, movement and behaviour. Birdwatchers call this 'jizz', and it is often enough to tell one bird from another.

Large birds that come to gardens include magpies and pigeons – woodpigeon, feral pigeon or collared dove. You may even spot a visiting sparrowhawk, although you are most likely to see everyday garden birds not birds of cliffs or remote forests. And you should expect to see summer birds in summer and winter birds in winter. But you never know. Look at the birds, bit by bit, and check their colours and patterns, including legs and beaks. Don't jump to conclusions, and read the descriptions in this guide, including when and where the bird can be expected. Above all, identify what you see only on the evidence before your own eyes.

Redwing
page 140

Robin
page 122

Starling
page 190

Sparrowhawk
page 46

How does it behave?

SOME BIRDS RUN, some walk, some hop, some shuffle. Some perch high in trees, some stay close to the ground, others cling to tree-trunks or climb straight up them. There are birds that are only ever seen singly or in pairs, and others which invariably feed, roost or travel in large flocks. Observing a bird's behaviour and habits may provide you with important clues to its identity.

HOUSE SPARROW *Moves on the ground by short hops, feeding in noisy groups and frequently taking dust baths.*

STARLING *Usually seen in flocks feeding on the ground – walking, running, probing for grubs, and squabbling.*

NUTHATCH *Moves in quick jerks – up, sideways or, uniquely, down on tree-trunks. Woodpeckers and treecreepers, by contrast, only climb upwards.*

MOORHEN *Swims high in the water and patters along the surface before taking off. In water, constantly flicks its tail, showing white tail patch.*

DUNNOCK *Shuffles or creeps like a mouse along the ground, with body held almost horizontal and legs almost hidden.*

MALLARD *Flies up almost vertically from the surface when alarmed; occasionally dives for food but more often simply dabbles and up-ends.*

LITTLE GREBE *Sometimes jumps with a splash before diving, or hides in the water by lowering its body until only its head still shows.*

Birds in flight

TO IDENTIFY A BIRD in the air, observe
whether its flight is fast and direct, or slow
and laboured; whether it zigzags or climbs
and falls in an undulating pattern; whether
it flaps, glides, soars or hovers. The angle at
which it holds its wings, and the wings' shape
and size, are also important. Other points to
look for include whether the bird shows any
distinctive wing or tail markings, and how
it holds its head and legs.

COLLARED DOVE
*Climbs high in the air then
falls in spring display flight;
can be told apart from
similar, smaller turtle dove
by under-tail pattern –
white tip is broader
than black base.*

SWIFT *Very fast flight with
rapid beats of long, scimitar-shaped
wings; frequently twists and turns
in the air, and alternates between
flapping and gliding.*

SWALLOW *Swoops
and wheels in the air
with easy, flowing
wing-beats, often low
over ground, catching
insects on the wing.*

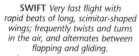

GREEN WOODPECKER *Combination of
green upperparts, brilliant yellow rump and
highly distinctive undulating flight; the bird
alternately rises and falls in the air, as it
flaps then closes its short, broad wings.*

ROOK *Direct and regular flight, with occasional gliding, often in loose, straggling flocks; wings are broad with deeply slotted tips.*

HERON *Flies slowly on down-curved wings, with head drawn well back, chest bulging and legs trailing behind.*

KESTREL *Hovers with tail fanned out and long, pointed wings holding it motionless against the wind; then dives on its prey.*

HOW BIRDS ARE GROUPED

SHAPE AND SIZE are the first clues to a bird's identity, whether you catch only a quick glimpse of the bird, or have time to study it in detail. Even if you cannot instantly put a name to the bird, its general appearance may at least suggest the family group to which it belongs. In this identification key, all the families of British birds that you are likely to see in a garden, from your garden or in a local park are described, and one species from each family is illustrated. Deciding to which family a bird belongs is a great aid to working out its species, since this narrows down the choice – often to relatively few birds. The information given about each family includes the habitat where the birds are most likely to be seen, and the size range of the species in each family. To complete an identification, refer to the main descriptions of birds on the pages indicated in the key.

Wildfowl Swans are the largest of the wildfowl, graceful in the water and powerful in the air. Geese are also large full-bodied birds with long necks and short legs. In almost all species of ducks, males are more boldly coloured than females. All wildfowl fly fast and powerfully, frequently maintaining formation.
SEE PAGES: *24-35*

Male

Mallard
page 28

Grebes Streamlined swimming and diving birds, with slender necks, very short tails and sharply pointed bills. They are clumsy on land, but expert in water. Flight is fast and direct.
SEE PAGES: *42-43*

Little Grebe
page 42

Gamebirds Heavy-bodied land birds, with stout, short bills, stubby, rounded wings, and strong legs and feet for scratching the ground for food. They often run – flight is fast and laboured, bursts of rapid wing beats alternating with brief glides.
SEE PAGES: *36-39*

Male

Pheasant
page 38

Grey heron
page 40

Herons Large wading birds with long necks and legs and long, sharp pointed bills. Their wings are broad and rounded. Flight is slow, with neck kinked and legs trailing behind.
SEE PAGES: *40-41*

Birds of prey All have sharp, hooked bills for tearing meat and strong feet armed with talons for killing and carrying prey. Masters of flight – some soar, some hover, some stoop or dive on prey, some fly prey down. Females usually larger than males.
SEE PAGES: *44-55*

Kestrel
page 50

Crakes and rails Medium sized or small long-legged birds, usually living on or near water, they prefer running or swimming to flying. Flight is usually laboured, with legs trailing behind. Crakes and rails are secretive.
SEE PAGES: *56-59*

Herring gull
page 64

Cuckoo
page 86

Cuckoos Our cuckoo is a long-tailed bird with long, pointed wings. Two toes point forwards, two backwards. In flight it can easily be mistaken for a small bird of prey.
SEE PAGES: *86-87*

Coot
page 58

Gulls Common seabirds, often found scavenging inland, with webbed feet and pointed wings. Plumage is usually grey, white and black. Males and females are alike; young birds are flecked with brown.
SEE PAGES: *60-69*

Pigeons Stout, rather heavy birds, with small heads and broad, pointed wings, angled at wrist. They often feed in flocks on the ground. Flight is rapid and powerful, with occasional gliding.
SEE PAGES: *70-79*

Owls Mainly night-hunting birds of prey, with round heads, half-hidden hooked beaks and large eyes. They fly silently, hunting for prey, and are most often seen at dusk.
SEE PAGES: *80-85*

Barn owl
page 80

Wood pigeon
page 70

Nightjars Our nightjar is a nocturnal insect-eater, with long wings and tail, short bill but wide gape and large, flat head. Flight is silent, smooth, wheeling.
SEE PAGES: *88-89*

Nightjar
page 88

Green woodpecker
page 94

Kingfishers Brilliantly coloured little bird with large head, short tail and long, sharp bill used to catch fish. Dives from perch, or hovers over water before it dive. Flight is fast and direct.
SEE PAGES: *90-91*

Kingfisher
page 90

Woodpeckers Colourful, broad-winged birds, with strong, sharp bills adapted for chipping and boring into tree trunks. Short, stiff tail is used for support when climbing trees. Flight is undulating.
SEE PAGES: *94-99*

Swift
page 102

Swifts Dark bird with long, curved wings, almost entirely aerial, flying fast to catch insects. Swifts are often seen in flocks, alternately flapping wings and gliding.
SEE PAGES: *102-103*

Larks Streaky, brown birds of open country, which nest and feed on the ground. Songs are usually delivered in flight. They often gather in flocks when the breeding season is over.
SEE PAGES: *104-105*

Skylark
page 104

Swallows and martins

Highly aerial small birds with long, pointed wings, forked tails, short legs and small feet. They are fast and graceful in flight, and use their wide mouths to catch insects in the air. Plumage is dark above and pale below. SEE PAGES: *106-111*

Swallow
page 106

Ring-necked parakeet
page 100

Parakeets Slender, long-winged, long-tailed, green birds with obvious slim parrot-like form and short, hooked beak. Makes screeching cries. Introduced into Britain.
SEE PAGES: *100-101*

Pipits and wagtails

Small, delicate, slender, long-tailed birds, with fine pointed bills adapted for catching insects. They feed mostly on the ground, running or walking. Flight is undulating.
SEE PAGES: *112-117*

Pied wagtail
page 114

Accentors The dunnock is a streaked, grey and brown bird, with sharp, thin insect-eater's bill. It usually feeds on the ground, moving with a mouselike shuffle, singing from an exposed perch.
SEE PAGES: *120-121*

Wren Tiny, active bird with short, barred brown tail held cocked upwards. Flight is rapid and direct, whirring on short, rounded wings.
SEE PAGES: *118-119*

Dunnock
page 120

Wren
page 118

Thrushes A diverse group of birds, ranging from small, warbler-like birds to the plump, long-legged thrushes. They feed mainly on the ground, eating insects, worms and fruit.
SEE PAGES: *122-141*

Blackbird
page 136

Long-tailed tits
A tiny, very long-tailed songbird, closely related to true tits. It is often found feeding in mixed flocks.
SEE PAGES: *162-163*

Long-tailed tit
page 162

Old world warblers
All warblers are slim, active, insect-eating birds, mostly with rather dull, brown plumage. Many species are shy and secretive, more likely to be heard than seen. A wide variety of songs helps to distinguish different species.
SEE PAGES: *142-157*

Treecreepers Ours is small, brown-backed, with a fine down-curved bill. It climbs spirally up tree trunks, probing the bark for insects, and is usually seen singly.
SEE PAGES: *176-177*

Pied flycatcher
page 160

Old world flycatchers
Small birds with rather flat, pointed bills, adapted for catching insects in the air. They perch very upright watching for insects, then dart to catch them.
SEE PAGES: *158-161*

Willow warbler
page 150

Treecreeper
page 176

Great tit
page 166

True tits Small, lively and acrobatic birds, many brightly coloured. In winter they often feed in mixed flocks.
SEE PAGES: *164-173*

Crows Largest of the perching birds, with broad wings and strong bills, legs and feet. Plumage is mostly black. Often found in flocks, they walk or hop on the ground.
SEE PAGES: *178-187*

Magpie
page 180

Nuthatch
page 174

Nuthatch A bird with a long, sharp bill for picking insects from the bark of trees. It can run down tree trunks as well as up them.
SEE PAGES: *174-175*

Waxwing
page 188

Waxwings Short-tailed, fruit-eating birds with highly distinctive crest on head. They are usually seen in flocks. Flight is fast and direct, similar to the flight of starlings.
SEE PAGES: *188-189*

Starling
page 190

Starlings Our species is a common, medium-sized bird, with speckled, dark plumage, sharp bill and short tail. Flight is rapid and direct. Flies, roosts and feeds in large flocks.
SEE PAGES: *190-191*

Finches Mostly small seed-eating birds with stout, heavy bills. Males are usually more brightly coloured than females. Often flock outside breeding season.
SEE PAGES: *196-213*

House sparrow
page 192

Sparrows Small, sturdy perching birds, with stout, strong bills for cracking seeds. They hop along the ground when feeding, and are highly gregarious.
SEE PAGES: *192-195*

Siskin
page 204

Buntings Similar to finches, with strong, stout bills; but feed mainly on the ground instead of in trees. Males are usually more brightly coloured than females.
SEE PAGES: *214-217*

Bullfinch
page 210

Reed bunting
page 214

Chaffinch
page 198

BIRDS

MUTE SWAN

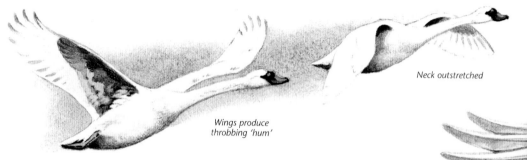

Neck outstretched

Wings produce throbbing 'hum'

IN POWERFUL FLIGHT, mute swans present a graceful spectacle and make an exciting, unmistakable sound – a throbbing 'wing music'. Britain's only resident swans, they are quieter than the migrant species but not entirely mute: they hiss and snort when angry, and can even honk weakly. The mute swan is the world's second heaviest flying bird – only slightly behind the Kori bustard of Africa – and can weigh 18kg. A serene appearance belies its aggressiveness when breeding.

Mute swan

Cygnus olor

152cm

| J | F | M | A | M | J |
| J | A | S | O | N | D |

Widespread in Britain and Ireland, except extreme north.

PARK WATCHING

Eager to take bread, mute swans are nevertheless wary and ready to threaten with intimidating postures the hand that feeds them. On water, stiffly arched wings and, on the land, an open bill and hoarse calls, warn you not to go much closer.

*Orange
bill with
black knob
at base*

*Curved
neck*

CANADA GOOSE

THE FIRST SPECIMENS of this very large goose were brought to Britain from Canada in the 17th century as decorative birds for parkland lakes. Later, attempts were made to increase their numbers as game birds; but the Canada goose is too tame and flies too low to make a sporting target. It has now spread out of its parkland homes, and its numbers are still increasing. The nest consists of plant material placed close to water, and is defended aggressively.

Long neck and deep wing-beats

Head lowered nearly to ground level in aggressive display when threatened

Birds stay in safe waters after breeding

Canada goose
Branta canadensis
90-100cm
J F M A M J
J A S O N D
Grassland by lakes, mainly in England.

White chin-patch

Black head
and neck

PARK
WATCHING

These geese are
beautiful to look at
but not ideal for a
small public park.
They can worry small
children, although
they are not really at
all dangerous, but
more importantly
they make a bit of a
mess with their large,
green droppings.
Enjoy them without
offering food.

Juvenile bird
has duller chin-patch
and more mottled
upper parts

MALLARD

IN TOWN AND COUNTRY, this is the most familiar duck in the British Isles. It is as much at home on a park lake or city canal as it is on a quiet country backwater or remote reservoir. Mallards in towns are very tame, but those in rural areas are wary, for they are much sought after by wildfowlers. Mallards are typical of dabbling ducks in that they feed on the water surface, or by up-ending, and spring straight up into the air from the water.

Males

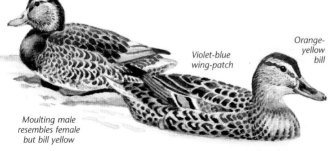

Moulting male resembles female but bill yellow

Violet-blue wing-patch

Orange-yellow bill

Female

Mallard

Anas platyrhynchos

58cm

J F M A M J
J A S O N D

Resident near water in all areas.

Green head

White collar

Yellow bill

Dark maroon-brown breast

Female

Occasionally mallards find quiet, secluded spots to nest in gardens: even in a sheltered flowerbed, or a thicket of cotoneaster. Mallard ducks can be remarkably bold and tolerant of disturbance, until the ducklings hatch and they make their way to the nearest water.

Pale belly, orange legs

Males pull back necks and flick water with bills in courtship displays

MANDARIN DUCK

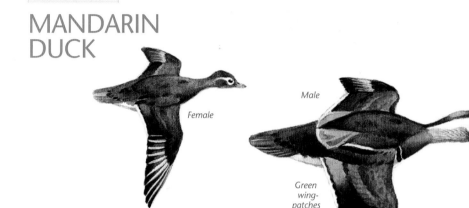

Female

Male

Green wing-patches

THIS WONDERFULLY PLUMAGED little duck is not a native of Europe, for it is an introduced species of 'perching duck' from eastern Asia that has managed to escape from captivity and establish itself as a breeding species. In this country mandarin ducks are to be found on large parkland lakes with well vegetated islands, and undisturbed tree-lined river banks. The nest is placed in holes in trees, or in nest-boxes. The male is unmistakable with his golden ruff and erectile, chestnut-orange wing-fans. Females are drab greyish-brown with whitish 'spectacles'.

PARK WATCHING

Parkland with old trees, where gnarled branches overhang lakes and streams and tree holes offer good nest sites, are ideal for mandarins. They are easily overlooked despite the male's colours and should be looked for in trees or in waterside rushes.

Mandarin duck

Aix galericulata

43cm

J F M A M J
J A S O N D

Breeds on lakes and rivers near trees, mainly in southern England.

White streak
on head

Whitish
'spectacles'

Golden
ruff

Female

Chestnut-orange
wing-fans

Male

RUDDY DUCK

THIS SPECIES IS A MEMBER of the stiff-tailed duck family, so called because of their habit of holding the tail erect. A native of North America, it was introduced into ornamental wildfowl collections and subsequently escaped into the wild. So successful were these escapees that ruddy ducks are well established as a British breeding species, and are still spreading. They inhabit ponds, lakes and reservoirs, especially those with reedy edges and other vegetation. Nests are woven platforms of vegetation, attached to reeds or other plants.

PARK WATCHING

This small duck is as often under water as on top when feeding, but spends long periods resting, half asleep, with its head tucked back and stiff tail cocked upwards. Even a sleeping male shows its white cheeks, but females are apt to be more puzzling.

A controversial cull is currently under way, aimed at killing all ruddy ducks in the UK. The justification for the cull is that the non-native ruddy duck is spreading to continental Europe where it could threaten the survival of the small, endangered western European population of the scarce white-headed duck by interbreeding and swamping its genes.

Plain wings

Male dark brown in winter

Ruddy duck

Oxyura jamaicensis

40cm

J F M A M J
J A S O N D

Breeds on vegetation-fringed lakes chiefly in central and southern England.

Brown cap

Stripe
on face

Female

Black cap and
very bright blue
bill; chestnut
body and
white face

Male in summer

TUFTED DUCK

A STRANGER TO BRITAIN before about 1840, the tufted duck is now the country's most common diving duck. These birds, which have become very tame, have been helped by the development of lakes from disused gravel pits and by the spread of reservoirs. The introduction of the zebra mussel, a favourite source of food, from Russia in the last century also encouraged their spread. Tufted ducks also eat small fish and insects. Males look black and white with a drooping crest; females are brown, with pale sides. In after-breeding plumage drakes become browner. Both sexes show a broad white wing-bar in flight.

Short, pointed wings

White sides

Tufted duck

Aythya fuligula

43cm

J F M A M J
J A S O N D

Widespread on fresh water; many immigrants in winter.

Male strikes 'bill down' pose after mating

Purple-black head and tuft

White wing-bar

Female

Male

PARK WATCHING

Park ponds and lakes are ideal for tufted ducks, which spread over the water and dive for food all day long. When they are sated, they gather in tight flocks and drift over the water surface, fast asleep. Look for the loose tufts on the males' heads.

RED-LEGGED PARTRIDGE

THIS GAME BIRD was first introduced deliberately into Britain in 1673, but the birds died out. Successful introductions date from 1770 when many eggs were brought in from France. Further imports occurred in the 19th and 20th centuries, and today the red-legged partridge greatly outnumbers native species. Although introduced for shooting purposes, the red-leg is not a particular favourite of hunters because of its reluctance to fly and preference to remain in cover, where its plumage helps it avoid detection. The nest is placed in vegetation on the ground. If two clutches of eggs are laid, the second just a few days after the first, the male has to care for one of the nests.

Birds prefer to seek safety in cover, not flight

White cheeks

GARDEN WATCHING

Should a partridge come into a garden, it is likely to be a red-legged: grey partridges stick to the open fields. Red-legs around farms perch more freely on fence posts, walls and even roofs, but only occasionally are they truly garden birds.

Red-legged partridge

Alectoris rufa

34cm

J F M A M J
J A S O N D

Heaths and farmland in central and southern England.

Rusty tail-sides
with greyish rump

Red bill

Black
throat
band and
shawl-like
streaks

Bright red legs

PHEASANT

THOUGH IT IS BRITAIN'S most wide-spread game bird the pheasant is not a native, for it was introduced from Asia in the Middle Ages. The rearing of pheasants for shooting has encouraged estate owners to maintain wooded habitats, so bringing benefit to other forms of wildlife. However, many foxes, crows and birds of prey have been killed to protect the pheasant from predators. The colourful and handsome male is distinctive with its long tail, iridescent blackish-green and violet head and metallic coppery sheen on its body, which is marked with dark crescents on breast and flanks.

GARDEN WATCHING

Pheasants are released for shooting and can still be tame during the following winter. They may then enter gardens and take advantage of food put out for other birds, especially seeds. They may reach up, or even flutter onto bird tables to take nuts and scraps.

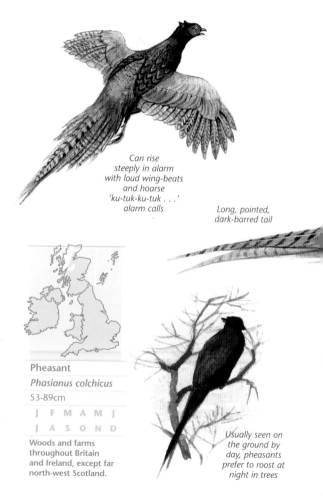

Can rise steeply in alarm with loud wing-beats and hoarse 'ku-tuk-ku-tuk . . .' alarm calls

Long, pointed, dark-barred tail

Pheasant

Phasianus colchicus

53-89cm

| J | F | M | A | M | J |
| J | A | S | O | N | D |

Woods and farms throughout Britain and Ireland, except far north-west Scotland.

Usually seen on the ground by day, pheasants prefer to roost at night in trees

Some males dark green;
some have white neck-ring

Red face

Dark green
head

Female smaller, shorter-
tailed and duller brown

Male

GREY HERON

ITS LARGE SIZE, long legs, and long sinuous neck make the grey heron unmistakable. Walking very slowly or poised, alert and motionless in or beside shallow water, this watchful bird waits patiently for a fish, frog or small mammal to come within range of its long, dagger-like bill. Then it stabs the prey and swallows it whole. Herons nest in colonies, usually in tall trees, but sometimes on cliffs and in reed-beds and bushes.

PARK WATCHING

Herons sometimes nest in trees or thickets on islands in park lakes, even in cities. Increasingly they are becoming bold around such pools, even queuing up for food: they prefer fish or scraps of meat to bread.

Huge broad wings flap slowly

Long legs trail behind tail

Neck drawn back and chest bulging in flight

Duller, greyer plumage overall including dusky neck

Adult early in breeding season; bills and legs brighter, with reddish tinges

Immature bird

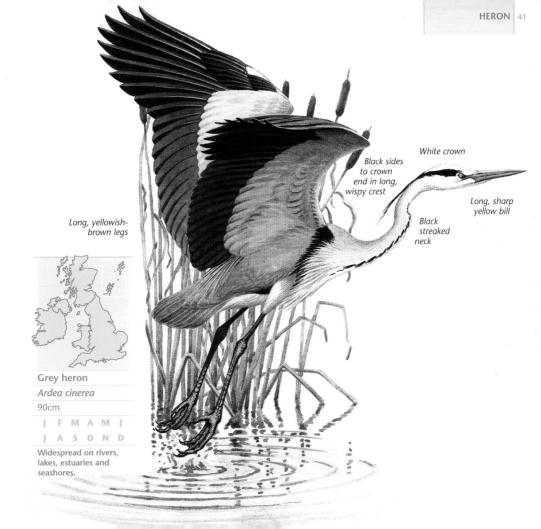

White crown

Black sides to crown end in long, wispy crest

Long, sharp yellow bill

Black streaked neck

Long, yellowish-brown legs

Grey heron

Ardea cinerea

90cm

J F M A M J
J A S O N D

Widespread on rivers, lakes, estuaries and seashores.

LITTLE GREBE

DURING ITS BUSY SEARCH for small
fish or water insects on reedy lakes
and rivers, the little grebe resembles
a small fluffy ball, diving frequently
and bobbing up again. It is often called
the dabchick, and is not much larger
than a duckling. Its nest is a floating
platform of water plants, often close
to the bank.

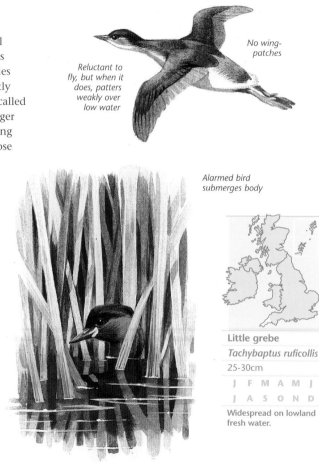

Reluctant to fly, but when it does, patters weakly over low water

No wing-patches

Alarmed bird submerges body

PARK WATCHING

A tiny, round-tailed,
small-billed bird
that bobs like a cork
and often plops
underwater is likely
to be a little grebe.
Listen for the long,
whinnying trill in
spring, a clue that
little grebes may be
nesting close by.

Little grebe

Tachybaptus ruficollis

25-30cm

J F M A M J
J A S O N D

Widespread on lowland
fresh water.

Winter

*Dull brown
above*

*Buffish
below*

*Like other grebes,
looks tail-less*

*Pale patch near
base of bill*

*Chestnut
throat*

Summer

RED KITE

THE CHILD'S TOY KITE was named after this bird because of its habit of soaring and swooping overhead. By the early 1900s gamekeepers – wrongly believing them to be a threat to their birds – had shot and poisoned them to the verge of extinction in Britain. Although strictly protected since 1903 their recovery was slow, and birds were confined as breeders to central Wales. Aided by reintroductions since 1989 in England and Scotland, numbers have now soared to around 1,000 pairs. Apart from carrion, the kite eats small mammals, birds and insects.

GARDEN WATCHING

Remarkably, red kites have been tempted in to gardens in places where they are common, coming down to take scraps of meat. This might revive bad habits – kites were once persecuted, as they were great chicken-run raiders.

Long wings, often held angled; white patches near tips

Pale,
finely
streaked
head

Male and
female look
similar

Red kite

Milvus milvus

60cm

J F M A M J
J A S O N D

Wooded hills in Wales,
Scotland and central
England; hunts over
moorland, in winter
over bogs and other
open country.

Long,
reddish,
forked
tail

SPARROWHAWK

A WATCHER MUST be alert to spot the quick flurry and chorus of frantic alarm calls as this yellow-eyed predator darts down a woodland ride or along a hedgerow, scattering terrified birds. Although most prey is captured with the advantage of surprise, the sparrowhawk is capable of overtaking a quarry by its sheer speed and agility. The nest is a flattened bulky platform of sticks, sometimes based on an old nest of another species. Males are much smaller than the females.

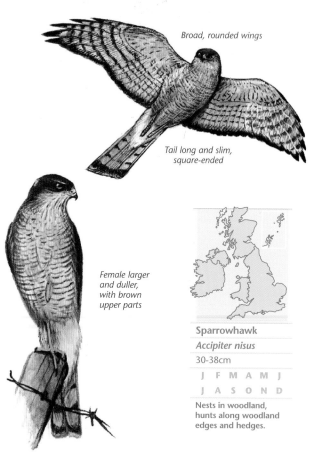

Broad, rounded wings

Tail long and slim, square-ended

Female larger and duller, with brown upper parts

GARDEN WATCHING

A sudden panic amongst the smaller birds might herald the arrival of a sparrowhawk. These small hawks ambush birds at garden feeders and often catch pigeons and doves and pluck them on the lawn: a brilliant but gory performance.

Sparrowhawk

Accipiter nisus

30-38cm

J F M A M J
J A S O N D

Nests in woodland, hunts along woodland edges and hedges.

Long yellow
legs

Male has
blue-grey
upper parts

Barred, reddish-
brown underparts
on male

BUZZARD

A FAMILIAR SOUND in hilly country in western and northern Britain is the loud mewing 'kiew' of a buzzard as it soars, apparently without effort, or hovers over a wooded hillside. This keen-sighted bird scans the ground for small mammals, especially rabbits and voles. Buzzards prefer open hillsides with wooded valleys and tall trees or cliffs on which to breed. They build a large nest of sticks which is decorated with greenery.

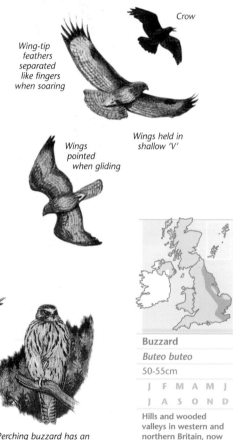

Crow

Wing-tip feathers separated like fingers when soaring

Wings held in shallow 'V'

Wings pointed when gliding

Finely barred tail

Perching buzzard has an upright stance and shows a heavy, rounded build

Buzzard

Buteo buteo

50-55cm

J F M A M J
J A S O N D

Hills and wooded valleys in western and northern Britain, now spreading into central and eastern England.

Broad, rounded wings, typically pale below with brown on forewings and trailing edge

GARDEN WATCHING

You will rarely see a buzzard in a garden, but, where they are common, you might well see one from a garden as it soars overhead. Listen for the challenging, whistling call, especially in spring, as buzzards defend their territories.

Short neck and broad head

Fan-like tail, with many narrow bars

KESTREL

A MEDIUM-SIZED, brownish falcon hovering above a roadside verge often catches the eye of the passing motorist – and usually means death for a vole or some other small mammal below. Lift-like, the bird drops by stages, finally pouncing and grasping with its talons. Kestrels, along with sparrowhawks, are Britain's most widespread birds of prey. They favour open country, but also flourish in urban areas with parks as well as motorway verges. They nest in holes in trees, tall buildings or nest-boxes. The adult male sports a russet back and wings, offset by a dove-grey crown and tail. Females are brown with dark spots.

Female is brown, heavily spotted above, with mainly rusty-brown tail

Young male has barred grey tail

Pairs sometimes breed in nest-boxes

Kestrel

Falco tinnunculus

34cm

J F M A M J
J A S O N D

All types of open country including urban areas; most numerous in rough grassland.

Long, usually
pointed wings

Dark outer
wing

Chestnut
back

Hovers over
ground

Grey tail
with black
band at tip

Male

GARDEN WATCHING

Kestrels are seen much less regularly in gardens than sparrowhawks, as they eat more mice and voles and fewer birds. Nevertheless, a hungry kestrel may sometimes make a dash for a sparrow, with a fair chance of success.

HOBBY

FOR SPEED, GRACE AND AGILITY in flight the hobby has few rivals, even among its fellow falcons. Whether delicately picking a dragonfly out of the sky, or swooping down to seize a swallow in full flight, it presents a breathtaking spectacle. Hobbies are great travellers, for they spend the winter in Africa before migrating north to breed in Britain. They lay their eggs in the old tree nest of a crow or large bird. The hobby's plumage is striking, and in flight its long wings, angled back, give it the appearance of a giant swift.

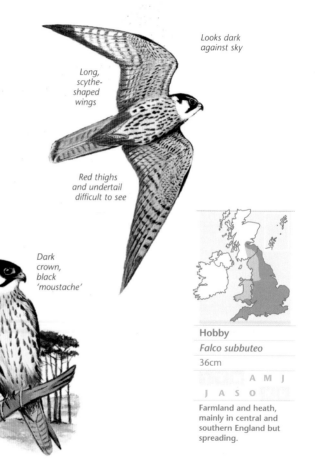

Looks dark against sky

Long, scythe-shaped wings

Red thighs and undertail difficult to see

Dark crown, black 'moustache'

Pale underparts streaked with black

Hobby

Falco subbuteo

36cm

A M J
J A S O

Farmland and heath, mainly in central and southern England but spreading.

Slate-coloured back

Shortish tail

Swift

GARDEN WATCHING

Hobbies will only come into exceptionally large gardens, with tall pine trees, but you might see them from your house. House martins forming tight, noisy flocks high overhead give away the deadly falcon's presence.

PEREGRINE FALCON

WHEN HUNTING, the peregrine is a mere speck in the sky as it keeps a lonely, circling watch for prey. When it sights its victim it suddenly snaps back its wings and dives towards it in a rapid 'stoop' estimated as reaching up to 180mph (290km/h). If contact is made the quarry – typically a pigeon or duck – is usually killed instantly as the falcon strikes it with its toes bunched.

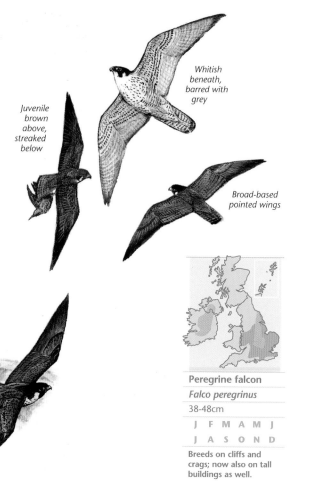

Whitish beneath, barred with grey

Juvenile brown above, streaked below

Broad-based pointed wings

Courting male loops the loop after mock dive at female

Peregrine falcon

Falco peregrinus

38–48cm

J F M A M J
J A S O N D

Breeds on cliffs and crags; now also on tall buildings as well.

Black and whitet cheek

Grey upperparts

Breeds mainly on high rock ledges

GARDEN WATCHING

Pigeons are classic peregrine food, so these falcons are becoming a more familiar sight around town and city centres. They do not normally enter gardens, but may soar overhead, keeping a sharp eye out for potential prey.

MOORHEN

IN SPITE OF ITS NAME this is not a moorland species; the name comes from the Anglo-Saxon *more*, meaning mere or bog. It eats water plants, insects, spiders, worms and other invertebrates which it picks from the surface or by up-ending. Like its cousin the coot it is aggressive in defence of its territory, attacking any encroaching neighbour with feet and bill. The feet are exceedingly long, but have no webbing, so its swimming action is jerky and laboured. If alarmed, the bird will dive and stay submerged with only its bill above the water. The nest is usually a woven structure, anchored to aquatic vegetation.

Chicks have bare red crown and blue patch above eye

Juvenile has dull brown body and pale throat and belly

Moorhen

Gallinula chloropus

33cm

J F M A M J
J A S O N D

Watersides of all sorts, from ponds and ditches to large lakes and rivers; often feeds in fields.

The moorhen, like the coot, needs a long pattering run to take-off

Dark brown
and black plumage

Bare red
forehead shield

White under
tail and flank
streak

**PARK
WATCHING**

This is a typical park
lake bird, creeping
around on waterside
grass or among the
rushes, or fluttering
away over the water
if disturbed. Look for
the rhythmic walk,
flicked tail and
bobbing head.

Green legs with
small red 'garter'

COOT

IN STRIKING CONTRAST to their black plumage, coots of both sexes have an area of bare skin on their forehead that matches their shiny white bill. Males squabble frequently over territory, with the white shield playing an important part in their aggressive displays. It is held forward, low on the water, with wings and body fluffed up behind, presenting a menacing impression. As two birds approach each other they produce an unmusical ringing call – rather like a hammer striking a steel plate. The coot's diet consists mainly of plant material for which it dives to bring to the surface to eat.

Long legs trail in flight

Juvenile has pale throat and breast

PARK WATCHING

A bird of more open water than the moorhen, the coot also feeds on areas of short grass, often in small flocks. On park ponds it is also liable to join the ducks and gulls in the noisy scramble for breadcrumbs.

Coot

Fulica atra

38cm

| J | F | M | A | M | J |
| J | A | S | O | N | D |

Large lakes and reservoirs, slow-moving rivers; feeds in fields; in winter also on estuaries.

Chicks have bare red and blue head with ruff of orange down

White bill
and forehead
shield

All-black
body

Large
lobed
feet

BLACK-HEADED GULL

THE NAME IS MISLEADING as this gull has a dark chocolate-brown hood in the breeding season only. This handsome smallish gull occurs abundantly inland as well as along our coasts. Indeed three-quarters of those in the British Isles nest inland around reservoirs, gravel pits or sewage farms – and especially on boggy areas near northern lakes. Only in the south does it breed mainly on the coast, often on salt-marshes or in sand-dunes. Flocks of black-headed gulls can be seen following the plough, picking up insects and worms. They are also a common sight on refuse tips in winter. Their harsh, rasping 'kee-arr' calls sound overpowering when a colony is in full cry.

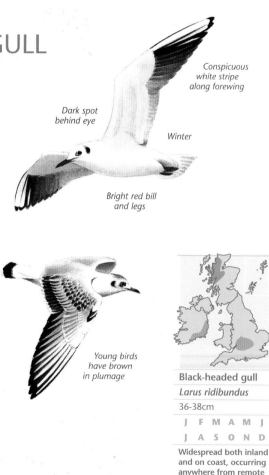

Conspicuous white stripe along forewing

Dark spot behind eye

Winter

Bright red bill and legs

Young birds have brown in plumage

GARDEN WATCHING

This is the commonest gull in gardens away from seaside towns (where the herring gull is more common). It also stands on town centre roofs and comes down to the streets to pick up scraps, or snatch insects from the ground.

Black-headed gull

Larus ridibundus

36-38cm

| J | F | M | A | M | J |
| J | A | S | O | N | D |

Widespread both inland and on coast, occurring anywhere from remote islands to city centres.

Dark chocolate-
brown hood

Dark
red bill

Flocks
follow
plough

Summer

Dark red
legs

COMMON GULL

THE COMMON GULL is, in fact, not nearly as common as a breeder as the name suggests, except in Scotland and western Ireland. Few breed in the southern half of Britain and eastern Ireland. However, it is common as a winter visitor. Its varied diet includes insects and worms, water creatures, other birds' eggs and young, and waste food at refuse tips. Sometimes it chases seabirds to steal food. The adult resembles a small herring gull with its grey back and white head, but the bill and legs are yellow-green; the wing-tips are black, with white spots or 'mirrors' (unlike the otherwise quite similar kittiwake). Its voice is a high-pitched mewing 'keeeyar'. The common gull nests in small colonies on rocks, islets or boggy areas of grass and moorland.

Head white

Summer

PARK WATCHING

This is not usually so common as some other gulls, but the loud, high-pitched, prolonged squealing calls draw attention to its presence around park lakes in winter. It is well worth looking for where gulls come to be fed.

Common gull

Larus canus

40cm

| J | F | M | A | M | J |
| J | A | S | O | N | D |

Breeds chiefly in Scotland and western Ireland; widespread in winter.

Head streaked grey-brown; dark eye gives gentle appearance

Black and white wing-tips

Winter

Yellow-green bill

Yellow-green legs

Back darker than herring gull

Common gulls sometimes pursue other seabirds to rob them of food

HERRING GULL

THE HARSH, LOUD 'kee-owk-kyowk-kyowk-kyowk' call of the commonest of our larger gulls evokes the very spirit of the seashore. It is heard at close quarters in coastal towns where the birds are increasingly breeding on rooftops. Although herrings may form part of its diet, it also eats shellfish, small mammals and birds and, like many other gulls, refuse from rubbish tips. Hard-shelled prey like mussels are dropped from a height to smash them. The similar yellow-legged gull has darker grey upperparts; it has become a regular visitor and a few pairs now nest in southern England.

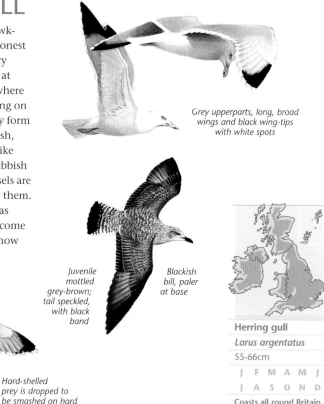

Grey upperparts, long, broad wings and black wing-tips with white spots

Juvenile mottled grey-brown; tail speckled, with black band

Blackish bill, paler at base

Hard-shelled prey is dropped to be smashed on hard ground below

Herring gull

Larus argentatus

55–66cm

J F M A M J
J A S O N D

Coasts all round Britain and Ireland; widespread inland, including towns and cities, in winter.

Red spot
on bill

Pale eye

Pink
legs

GARDEN & PARK WATCHING

In some towns herring gulls nest on flat rooftops. Elsewhere, it is not much of a garden bird, but always likely to be the commonest big gull in the scrum for food around town centre riversides and park lakes.

Young take four years to acquire full adult plumage

LESSER BLACK-BACKED GULL

Dark grey upper parts

Slender build

THIS HANDSOME BIRD is about the same length as the herring gull, but with a slimmer build and darker grey back and upperwings. These are slate grey in the race breeding in Britain and Ireland, while in the race breeding in Scandinavia and western Russia – which is a common winter visitor here, they are blackish, though not quite as black as the wingtips. They can be distinguished from the great black-backed gull by their smaller size, smaller head and slimmer bill.

First-year bird is darker than herring gull

Lesser black-backed gull

Larus fuscus

53-55cm

J F M A M J
J A S O N D

Breeds mainly in north and west. Found both on coast and inland, including urban areas.

Grey back darker than herring gull

Large winter roosts form on inland waters

Head streaked in winter

Varied diet includes crabs

GARDEN & PARK WATCHING

Flat roofs in industrial areas and coastal towns attract lesser black-backed gulls to nest in many places, but otherwise this big bird is not really a garden bird. Look for it around town park lakes and riverside embankments.

Yellow legs

GREAT BLACK-BACKED GULL

THE GREAT BLACK-BACKED gull is the world's largest species of gull. It has benefited from a reduction in persecution by people, the gradual warming of the North Atlantic and to the increase in edible refuse thrown away by man. It eats refuse, carrion, crabs and fish, but it is also a powerful predator that regularly preys on adult birds and chicks of other species, including puffins, shearwaters and kittiwakes. It has very deep, hoarse, barking calls.

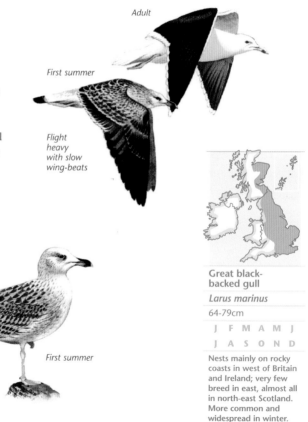

Adult

First summer

Flight heavy with slow wing-beats

First summer

Paler head than immature lesser black-backed; great size and heavy bill also distinguish it

Great black-backed gull

Larus marinus

64-79cm

J F M A M J
J A S O N D

Nests mainly on rocky coasts in west of Britain and Ireland; very few breed in east, almost all in north-east Scotland. More common and widespread in winter.

Long, broad wings

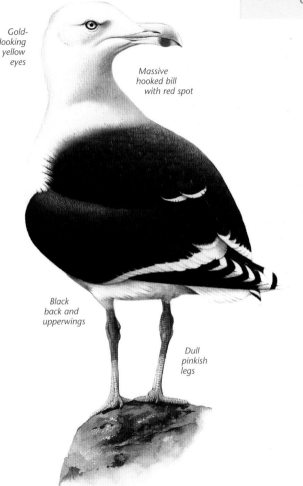

Gold-looking yellow eyes

Massive hooked bill with red spot

Black back and upperwings

Dull pinkish legs

GARDEN & PARK WATCHING

Gulls on park lakes can include several species, but the great black-backed is usually rather scarce. It is also the biggest and most aggressive. It may stand on the ridge of a rooftop in an industrial area together with smaller relatives.

WOODPIGEON

TO MANY FARMERS, the largest of Britain's pigeons is 'public enemy number one'. The woodpigeon does immense damage to crops, particularly in winter when the population is joined by continental immigrants, and huge flocks feed on rape, other brassicas and clover – plentiful alternatives to their traditional foods of ivy berries, acorns and weed seeds. At other times of the year they feed on cereals, potatoes, beans, peas and greens. The woodpigeon is distinguished from other pigeons by its white neck-patch and wing-patches, the latter conspicuous in flight. The lovely song is a soft, husky cooing, 'coo-coo, coo, coo . . . cuk'. In display flight the bird climbs steeply, noisily claps its wings together and then glides down.

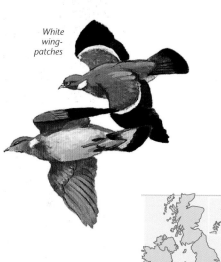

White wing-patches

GARDEN WATCHING

Woodpigeons are often unwelcome on garden bird tables, being so big, greedy and often messy, but they do make an impressive sight. More appealing, they visit garden elders and ivy, to take buds, flowers and berries in season.

Woodpigeon

Columba palumbus

40cm

| J | F | M | A | M | J |
| J | A | S | O | N | D |

Most on arable farmland near woods, but breeds everywhere except on high ground; residents joined by immigrants in winter.

White neck-patch
on adult (lacking
on juvenile)

Pinkish
breast

Broad black
band at
end of tail

STOCK DOVE

THIS PLUMP DOVE is basically all grey with two black bars on the wing, and a greenish neck-patch. It nests in holes in trees and rock faces and old buildings and, very occasionally, in disused rabbit burrows. A similar species breeding in remote coastal areas of Ireland and northern Scotland is called the rock dove. This is most readily distinguished from the farmland-dwelling stock dove by its white rump. Most pigeons found in urban areas are descended from a domesticated form of the rock dove, even though few resemble the wild bird in plumage. They roost on buildings instead of cliffs, and are often known as feral, town or London pigeons.

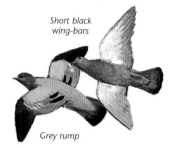

Short black wing-bars

Grey rump

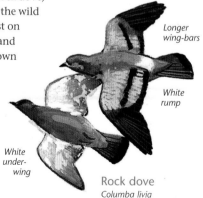

Longer wing-bars

White rump

White under-wing

Rock dove
Columba livia

Stock dove

Columba oenas

33cm

J F M A M J

J A S O N D

Breeds widely in woods and cliffs; often feeds on arable farmland.

No white on neck or wings

Blue-grey body

Small dark wing spots

Coral-red legs

GARDEN & PARK WATCHING

Look for this smaller, neater relative of the woodpigeon in parks where there are old trees, or crumbling ruins, with cavities where stock doves can nest. Listen for the deep, rhythmic cooing song.

FERAL PIGEON

THE FAMILIAR TOWN CENTRE pigeon is by far the most common bird in urban areas, but you are just as likely to see it on a coastal cliff, in a mountainside quarry or feeding on grain in country fields. It is a descendant of the wild rock pigeon, domesticated centuries ago for food and sport. Many of these tamed pigeons 'go wild' (or feral) instead of returning to their lofts or dovecotes, and many thousands now live as wild birds. That many still 'escape' is obvious from the number in our towns that sport coloured, numbered leg rings: these are 'racers' that have failed to make it back home.

Pigeons may be anything from white to black, via various patterns of blue-grey and chestnut brown. But after a few generations they tend to revert to the blue-grey of the wild rock dove, often with a white patch on the back and black bars across each wing. A fleshy, bare patch on the bill, called the 'cere', tends to be larger on feral birds than on wild ones. Otherwise, the pigeons behave much like their ancestors.

Once food is discovered, flocks quickly collect

Typical 'racing pigeon' shape, with small, bullet head and pointed wings. White rump is a throwback to wild ancestors, but often absent on feral birds

Feral pigeon

Columba livia

31–34cm

| J | F | M | A | M | J |
| J | A | S | O | N | D |

Widespread in Britain and Ireland except in forested areas.

Red eye

Rounded head

Pointed wingtips

GARDEN & PARK WATCHING

Despite attempts to prevent them doing it, town pigeons frequently perch on statues and town centre buildings, but less often in trees or on wires. They come freely to be fed in towns, but become quite wary and unapproachable where they live in open fields.

Short red legs

Small, fleshy white patch above beak

COLLARED DOVE

BEFORE THE 1930S the range of the collared dove in Europe was largely restricted to parts of the Balkans. Since then, in an amazing population explosion, it has colonised much of Europe as far north as Iceland. By 1955 it was nesting in Britain, and it has now colonised almost the entire British Isles. Favourite habitats are in the vicinity of farms, chicken runs, corn mills and docks, where grain and other animal feed is often spilled, and in gardens where birds are fed. The birds nest mainly in conifers, and can produce five broods – each of one or two young – between March and November. The song is a loud, monotonously repeated 'coo-coo-cuk'.

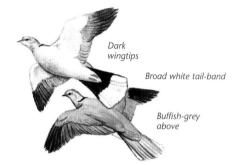

Dark wingtips

Broad white tail-band

Buffish-grey above

GARDEN WATCHING

If you listen carefully you will find the triple cooing song of this delicate dove is more varied than you might initially imagine: the wheezy, emphatic flight call is unique, too. Try to tell the youngsters with no collars from their neater parents.

Collared dove

Streptopelia decaocto

32cm

J F M A M J
J A S O N D

Widespread, except for uplands and city centres.

Frail nest of twigs sometimes built low among brambles

No collar on
young bird

Black half-collar
on nape of neck

Buffish-
grey body

TURTLE DOVE

THE THROBBING, PURRING coo of
the turtle dove is a bird call of high
summer that mingles well with the
sound of cricket on the village green.
This dove visits Britain in summer
from its winter quarters in sub-
Saharan Africa. Adults sport a heavily
chequered black and chestnut back and
a black and white half-collar, while the
underparts have a pinkish tinge. In
flight the undertail shows a rounded
white tip. Juveniles are duller. Sadly
this lovely bird has suffered massive
declines over the past 30 years.

GARDEN WATCHING

Garden bird tables will not usually attract
this scarce farmland dove, but it is possible
that one might perch on an overhead wire,
or purr its spring song from a nearby tall,
dense hedge.

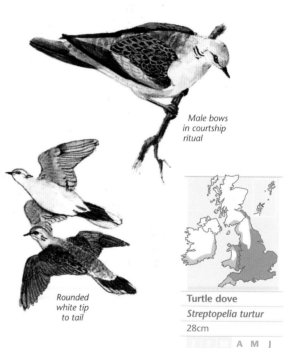

*Male bows
in courtship
ritual*

*Rounded
white tip
to tail*

Turtle dove

Streptopelia turtur

28cm

			A	M	J
J	A	S			

**Open woodlands
and tall, dense hedges,
mainly in southern
and eastern England.**

Chestnut and
black above

Black and
white neck-patch

Pink
breast

BARN OWL

A WHITE SHAPE silently leaving a barn or quartering a field is all an observer often sees of the barn owl. A closer view reveals golden-buff upperparts lightly mottled with grey, a white heart-shaped face with dark eyes, white underparts and long white-feathered legs. The barn owl feeds mostly on rats, mice and voles, which it catches mainly at night. It breeds in barns, ruins and church towers, and also in natural sites such as cliff holes and hollow trees. This very beautiful bird has suffered a huge decline, due to intensification of agriculture, poisoning by rodenticides and lack of natural nest sites as old trees are felled and traditional barns converted to housing.

Hollow elm trees are a favourite nest site but they are fast disappearing from the countryside

Wings spread out in threat display to defend owlets from intruder

Barn owl

Tyto alba

34cm

J F M A M J
J A S O N D

Widespread but local in agricultural country, but scarce in north-east England, upland Scotland and north-west Ireland.

White face

Ghostly all-white appearance in flight

Golden-buff upperparts

GARDEN WATCHING

Big, open gardens backing onto fields and paddocks may appeal to a barn owl: a nestbox can be successful, in an old tree or a big outbuilding. Only where natural food is plentiful can you expect to see one, though.

White underparts

Long legs

LITTLE OWL

THE SMALLEST of our breeding owls was introduced to this country from the Continent in the late 19th century. Although mainly nocturnal, it can be seen in daylight, especially on warm summer evenings. The birds breed in holes and crevices, and frequent agricultural land, parks, orchards, quarries and sea-cliffs. Insects, small birds and mammals form the main part of the little owl's diet. Its main calls are a plaintive 'kiew', and a yelping 'werrrow'.

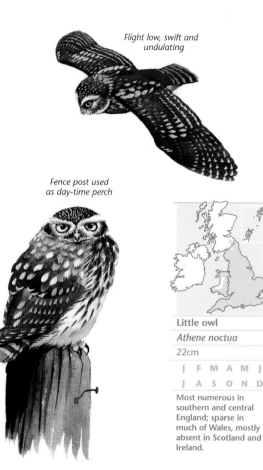

Flight low, swift and undulating

Fence post used as day-time perch

Like adults, fledglings bob heads when anxious

Little owl

Athene noctua

22cm

J F M A M J
J A S O N D

Most numerous in southern and central England; sparse in much of Wales, mostly absent in Scotland and Ireland.

Plumage grey-
brown and white

GARDEN
WATCHING

Watch over large
gardens and parks,
to fields and open
areas with scattered,
old trees and walls for
this small, rounded
owl. Listen for its
loud, yapping call,
especially on spring
and autumn evenings.

'Frowning'
expression
due to white
eyebrows

Yellow eyes

TAWNY OWL

THE MALE'S LONG, quavering, 'hoo-hoo-hoo-hooooo', often described as 'to-whit-to-wooo' incorporating the 'ke-wick' call of a responding female, is known to most people more from films and television than from hearing the real thing. During the day, the tawny owl's presence is often given away by the alarm calls of small birds mobbing an adult dozing on the branch of a tree. Its wholly dark eyes distinguish the tawny owl (sometimes called the brown owl) from other owls. As with other owls, soft plumage and specially adapted wing feathers make it silent in flight.

Fledglings have barred downy underparts

GARDEN WATCHING

Big nest boxes in ivy-covered trees can help tawny owls in large gardens and wooded parks. If people leave well alone all is well, but tawny owls may attack intruders who interfere with the nest: their silent approach makes them dangerous.

Big rounded face

Tawny owl

Strix aluco

38cm

J F M A M J
J A S O N D

Woodlands throughout Britain; absent from Ireland; occurs in farmland with trees, large gardens and city parks as well as large woods.

Brown body
with dark streaks
below

Hunts
after
dark

Dark
eyes

Owl watches for prey
from tree perch, then
pounces without
warning

CUCKOO

THE FAMILIAR 'CUC-COO, CUC-COO' call of the male bird in April is a sure sign that summer is on its way. The female has a very different loud bubbling call. Cuckoos are notorious for their parasitic breeding habits. The female finds suitable nests, built by much smaller birds, in which to lay her eggs. One egg is deposited in each nest after the cuckoo has carefully removed one of the host's eggs. The nests of meadow pipits, dunnocks and reed warblers are mostly chosen. Individual cuckoos parasitise particular species. When hatched the young cuckoo ejects the remaining eggs or nestlings of the host.

GARDEN WATCHING

Listen for the first cuckoo calling unmistakably in April. Visitors to gardens are rare, but you might see and hear a brown juvenile, calling constantly to be fed by any passing bird, in June or July.

Adult

Long, pointed wings

Grey-brown juvenile

White nape spot

White tip to tail

Slightly broader wings

Reed warbler feeds hungry young cuckoo

Newly hatched cuckoo ejects host bird's eggs

Reed warbler drives off cuckoo

Female cuckoo removes egg from host nest

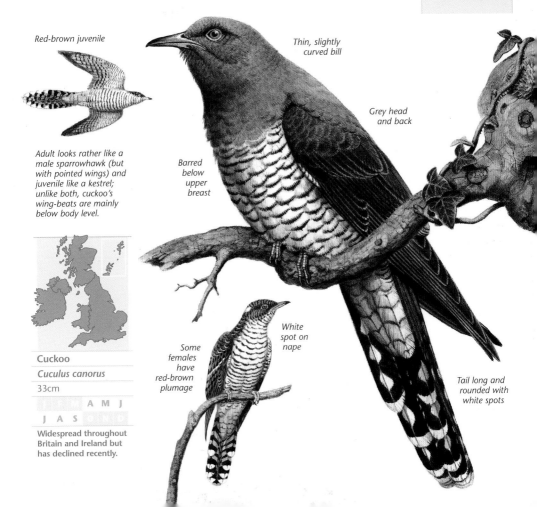

Red-brown juvenile

Adult looks rather like a male sparrowhawk (but with pointed wings) and juvenile like a kestrel; unlike both, cuckoo's wing-beats are mainly below body level.

Thin, slightly curved bill

Grey head and back

Barred below upper breast

White spot on nape

Some females have red-brown plumage

Tail long and rounded with white spots

Cuckoo

Cuculus canorus

33cm

J F M **A M J J A S O** N D

Widespread throughout Britain and Ireland but has declined recently.

NIGHTJAR

Nightjar perches along branch, not across it

May be seen feeding or displaying at dusk. Wings and tail look very long and flight is light and agile, with sudden long glides, twists and turns and brief hovering

THE NIGHTJAR'S CHURRING, long drawn-out song, uttered at night, rises and falls in pitch. It is most often seen at dusk when it hawks for flying insects such as large moths, which it catches in a huge open gape. The bird is also known as the 'goatsucker' from the old (but erroneous) belief that it milks goats with its large mouth. Nightjars are localised summer visitors, that have suffered major declines in the past 70 years.

Female

Nest is a scrape in the ground, with parent, eggs and young camouflaged among sticks and dead leaves

No white spots on tail or wings

Tiny bill but wide
hair-fringed gape

Intricately patterned
grey-brown plumage

Nightjar

Caprimulgus europaeus

27cm

J A S O M J

Heaths, moors and
open woodland, mainly
in southern England
and East Anglia.

During display
flight male
claps his wings
together audibly
over his back

Male

Bright white tail-spots
and wing-spots

**GARDEN
WATCHING**

The distant churring of a nightjar might be
audible from your garden if you live close to
a heath. Watch for nightjars feeding at or after
dusk, hawking for moths in a mysterious,
wheeling, buoyant flight.

KINGFISHER

A FLASH OF IRIDESCENT blue speeding along the river bank is the most that many people see of the stunningly coloured kingfisher. A closer view shows blue-green upper parts, orange cheeks and orange underparts. The bird has a white throat and neck patch, tiny red feet and a long, dark, dagger-like bill. It perches on a branch, watching for small fish. When a suitable prey is spotted, the bird dives into the water and catches its victim in its bill. The kingfisher returns to its perch, beats the fish against the branch to kill it, then swallows it head first. Both adults dig a long tunnel in the river bank to make their nest.

White tip to beak of young

Juveniles duller, with a white bill tip and duller legs

Adult feeds young bird

Nest is in tunnel dug in river bank

Vivid blue back

Short wings and tail

After making a capture, the kingfisher beats the fish against the branch

Iridescent blue-green above

Dagger-like bill

Orange-chestnut below

Red feet

Kingfisher

Alcedo atthis

16.5cm

J F M A M J
J A S O N D

Along slow-moving rivers; scarce in Scotland.

GARDEN & PARK WATCHING

Early morning is the best time to see a kingfisher on a visit to a garden pond: it will come in, take a fish and be gone before anyone is about to disturb it. The same goes for the park lake: it is best to look when few people are about.

HOOPOE

WHEN ERECTED, the long, black-edged crest of the hoopoe is unmistakable. This is a bird that spends winter in Africa and migrates to southern and central Europe in summer. A very few birds extend their journey northwards to southern England. Surprisingly for such a boldly marked bird it can be difficult to see when perched or when feeding on the ground. In flight, which is undulating with lazy flaps on broad, rounded wings, the striking appearance is unmistakable. The song is a low 'poo-poo-poo', often repeated and far-carrying.

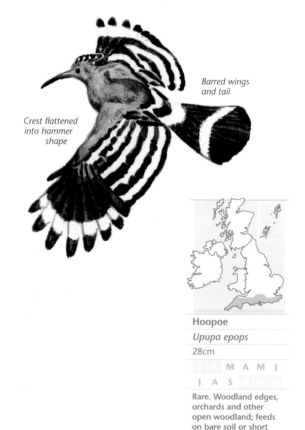

Crest flattened into hammer shape

Barred wings and tail

GARDEN WATCHING

This is a rare visitor to Britain in spring: you would be exceptionally lucky to see one at all, but if you have a big, open lawn, your find of a lifetime might happen in your own garden. Dreams can come true . . .

Hoopoe

Upupa epops

28cm

| | | M | A | M | J |
| J | A | S | | | |

Rare. Woodland edges, orchards and other open woodland; feeds on bare soil or short grass (including lawns).

Black-edged crest raised in alarm or when alighting

Long down-curved bill; feeds on insects and grubs

Pink-brown body

GREEN WOODPECKER

THE LOUD, RINGING 'kew-kew-kew' call of this largest of British woodpeckers sounds like laughter and gives this bird the local country name of 'yaffle'. It is brightly and distinctively coloured. Both sexes have the black face-patch; the female has a black 'moustache', which on the male is red and black-edged. The green woodpecker seldom 'drums' like its two spotted relatives. And unlike them, it feeds mainly on the ground, using its dagger-like bill to hack into short grass to extract ants and their eggs, larvae and pupae from their nests.

The adult female has a black 'moustache'. Juveniles have pale-spotted upperparts and dark spotted and barred underparts

GARDEN & PARK WATCHING

Any wide expanse of grass – such as a big lawn in a park or garden – will attract this ground-feeding woodpecker. It will search avidly for ants. Should you disturb it, look for the greenish-yellow rump as it flies away.

Longish, powerful
tapering bill

Red
crown

Red 'moustache'
edged in black
(all-black on female)

Green
back

Vivid greenish-
yellow rump,
conspicuous
in flight

Green woodpecker

Picus viridis

32cm

J F M A M J
J A S O N D

Widespread in woods
in England and Wales,
spreading in Scotland;
not in Ireland.

Male

GREAT SPOTTED WOODPECKER

RAPID BLOWS with its bill on a dead branch produce the characteristic drumming sound of a great spotted woodpecker establishing territory. It is also known as the pied woodpecker because of its mainly black and white plumage. The large white shoulder patches are easily recognised. Both sexes have bright red under-tail patches, but only the male has a red patch on the nape. Young birds have a red cap.

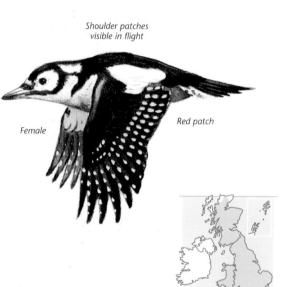

Shoulder patches visible in flight

Female

Red patch

GARDEN WATCHING

This is the woodpecker that comes regularly to peanut baskets: only thrush-sized, it is not very big, but its colouring is spectacular, making it hard to miss. Hang out lumps of fat or cheese for your woodpeckers.

Great spotted woodpecker

Dendrocopos major

23cm

J F M A M J
J A S O N D

Widespread in woods and other areas with trees, including town gardens and parks, but not in Ireland.

Red nape
on male

White
shoulder
patches

Male

Red
undertail

LESSER SPOTTED WOODPECKER

ONLY THE SIZE of a house sparrow, the lesser spotted woodpecker can be elusive among the top branches of trees where it likes to live. Its other name, the barred woodpecker, better describes its plumage; the black upper parts are barred with white. The male's cap or crown is red, the female's buff. The bird drums in spring; each burst is longer, softer, yet more rattling than that of the great spotted woodpecker.

Young bird brownish on head

Female has buff cap

The lesser spotted woodpecker often nests in orchards and rural parkland

GARDEN WATCHING

This finch-sized woodpecker is extremely rare on hanging feeders, but it will explore old apple trees in gardens, flitting through the branches and being surprisingly elusive. You might hear the high-pitched *pee-pee-pee-pee-pee* call in spring.

Lesser spotted woodpecker

Dendrocopos minor

14.5cm

J F M A M J
J A S O N D

Woods and hedgerows in England and Wales; not in Scotland or Ireland.

Black and
white pattern
noticeable
in flight

Red cap

White bars
on black
back

Male

No red
beneath tail

RING-NECKED PARAKEET

IN MANY CITIES, from Cairo to London, the ring-necked parakeet has been introduced, or has established after escapes from aviaries. A bird of tropical woodland, it likes the mild conditions of Kent and Surrey, where hundreds may roost together. Supported by the peanuts and sunflower seeds offered to smaller garden birds, parakeet numbers have steadily increased and the birds may become pests, especially to fruit growers. They compete with native birds such as stock doves and starlings for suitable nest holes in trees.

The birds are hard to mistake, but away from regular areas they could be confused with another similar species that may have escaped. The male ring-necked, or rose-ringed, parakeet is a clear green with a ring of pink-red around the neck and a small black bib; females lack the neck ring. They have long, narrow wings and elongated, pointed tails, obvious in the fast, direct flight. They draw attention with their loud, screeching calls.

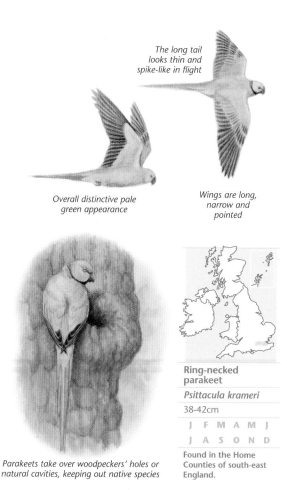

The long tail looks thin and spike-like in flight

Overall distinctive pale green appearance

Wings are long, narrow and pointed

Parakeets take over woodpeckers' holes or natural cavities, keeping out native species

Ring-necked parakeet

Psittacula krameri

38-42cm

J F M A M J
J A S O N D

Found in the Home Counties of south-east England.

Green body

Small, hooked, rose-red bill

Thin collar on male

GARDEN & PARK WATCHING

Listen for the screech of a passing parakeet and look quickly for the fast-flying bird: although it is as long as a pigeon, it is slim and long-tailed, and my look smaller than you expect. It feeds acrobatically, supporting itself with its strong feet and hooked beak.

Pointed tail shows pale yellow and bluish-green

Two toes forward, two back, like a woodpecker's foot

SWIFT

FEW BIRDS SPEND more of their lives in the air than the swift. They collect all their food and nesting material in flight, and drink and bathe without alighting. Swifts even mate on the wing, and at dusk parties of them can be seen circling higher and higher into the sky to spend the night 'cat-napping' while airborne. Insects are funnelled into the large gape with the help of stiff bristles around the mouth. Food for the young is stored in a throat pouch which can often be seen bulging with gorged insects. Alighting only to nest and feed the young, the swift breeds in holes and crevices in cliffs and buildings.

Screaming mobs dash around rooftops

Often nests in gaps in stonework under roofs

Swift

Apus apus

16.5cm

			A	M	J
	J	A	S		

Widespread visitor, except in north-west Scotland.

Flocks circle higher at dusk

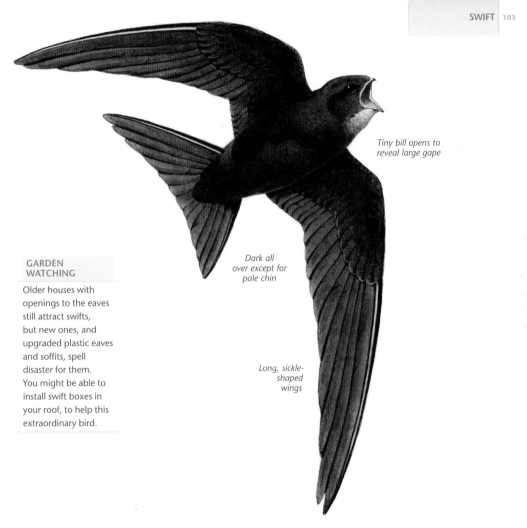

Tiny bill opens to reveal large gape

Dark all over except for pale chin

Long, sickle-shaped wings

GARDEN WATCHING

Older houses with openings to the eaves still attract swifts, but new ones, and upgraded plastic eaves and soffits, spell disaster for them. You might be able to install swift boxes in your roof, to help this extraordinary bird.

SKYLARK

AS IT FLIES ABOVE the open fields and downs, giving voice loudly, the skylark is a difficult bird to ignore. It breeds more widely in Britain than any other bird, occurring on all types of open habitats including farmland, grassland, meadows, commons and sand-dunes. It is larger than the woodlark and has a plainer face and a bigger crest. Rising almost vertically in a hovering flight, often to several hundred feet, the skylark sustains its clear warbling song for several minutes, before sinking gradually to the ground, still singing. Sadly, this much loved bird has suffered major declines over the past 25 years, due to agricultural intensification.

Migrant skylarks on open sand-dunes

Song sustained while in flight, often when hovering

Tail longer than woodlark's

Skylark

Alauda arvensis

18cm

J F M A M J
J A S O N D

Widespread; joined by migrants from northern and eastern Europe in winter.

GARDEN WATCHING

Skylarks are likely to settle only in larger gardens, and then only in hard weather, for they do not like the vicinity of trees or even bushes. You will notice the steady, even walk and half-crouch of the lark, which does not hop like a finch.

Crest may be lowered or raised

Dark-streaked brown upperparts and breast and off-white below

Longish tail with white outer feathers

Long hind claws typical of larks

SWALLOW

ALTHOUGH SWALLOWS are regarded as harbingers of summer, the first birds often arrive from their African wintering grounds as early as March. Swallows rarely land on the ground except to gather nest material. They hunt and drink on the wing, skimming over the water. Their pleasant, twittering song is often heard as they perch on telephone wires. The swallow's russet throat and the long tail streamers of the adults (longest in males) are unmistakable. Swallows usually nest in barns, stables and other buildings, frequently returning to the same locality, even the exact site, to breed. The nest is a cup of mud and straw, typically on a ledge or rafter.

Before migration, swallows often gather in large numbers on telegraph wires

Graceful flight with constant swooping and changes of direction; fluid beats of broad-based pointed wings alternating with glides

Russet throat and forehead in both sexes

Swallow

Hirundo rustica

19cm

| | | | M | A | M | J |
| J | A | S | O | | | |

Widespread in open country, near buildings for nesting and usually water.

Swallows drink on the wing

The young are fed with insects by both parents. They usually fly about three weeks after hatching; the relatively long fledging period is common among birds that nest in secure places

Upperparts blue-black in both sexes

White band across tail

Female

Shorter tail streamers

Male

Longer tail streamers

Young have duller, paler orange-buff forehead and throat and short tail streamers

GARDEN WATCHING

Open sheds, car ports, barns and other outbuildings are essential for nesting swallows: at least an open window is needed to gain access to the sheltered interior. Swallows love to perch on overhead wires and television aerials.

In high summer, swallows capture much of their food in low-level flight

HOUSE MARTIN

A SHORT TAIL and a white rump distinguish the house martin from the swallow. Traditionally it is a cliff-nesting species, but it has adapted to nesting under house eaves. Its nest of mud and plant fibres is cup-shaped, with only a small entrance at the top. Arriving from Africa in April or May, house martins start breeding almost immediately and raise two or even three broods each year. The birds swoop and wheel to catch flying insects for food. Nests built by house martins that arrive early are often re-used by later migrants.

Nests in small colonies

A thousand or more little pellets of mud are gathered to make the cup-shaped nest

House martin

Delichon urbica

12.5cm

| | | | A | M | J |
| J | A | S | O | | |

Widespread in and around villages and towns, and farmland; scarce in north and west Scotland and western Ireland.

White underparts and bold white rump

Blue-black upper parts

GARDEN WATCHING

House martins need mud as much as they need insects if they are to nest successfully: a muddy-edged garden pond is ideal. They are the ones that make round cups of mud under the eaves and flutter over the rooftops all summer.

Insects are caught in flight

Tail less forked than swallow's

SAND MARTIN

THE SAND MARTIN population is prone to fluctuations caused by the weather in its African winter quarters. Periodic droughts drastically reduce the numbers of aerial insects on which the birds feed. Slightly smaller than the house martin, the sand martin takes its name from its nesting habits: it digs out a 35-120cm long tunnel in a sand-bank, leading to a nesting chamber lined with plant material and feathers. In good weather years, sand martins may raise two broods.

Feet are used to dig out nest tunnel in sand

Sand martins roost in reed-beds

Sand martin

Riparia riparia

12cm

M A M J
J A S

Widespread where there are sandy banks for nesting, usually by rivers or in sand or gravel pits.

White underparts with brown breast-band

GARDEN & PARK WATCHING

A park lake may attract sand martins to feed over the water, as they take tiny insects in mid air and like watery places. They may nest nearby if there is a steep cliff of sand or soft sandstone into which they can tunnel.

Tail less forked than house martin's

All-brown upper parts

MEADOW PIPIT

PRESENT ALL YEAR in the countryside although many migrate south for winter, the meadow pipit is a bird of open country and not a common visitor to small gardens. Its long hind claws and more densely streaked breast, and its thinner 'eest' or 'tissip' call, distinguish this bird from the tree pipit. The conspicuous song flight by the male starts as the bird flies up to 30m from the ground, uttering an accelerating series of 'pheet' notes. These reach a climax and are replaced by slower and more liquid notes as the bird 'parachutes' down.

Long tail, white-edged

'Parachuting' song flight starts and ends from ground

GARDEN & PARK WATCHING

This small, streaky, creeping bird can be a secretive visitor to more open gardens, but is more likely to be seen in a large, open, grassy park. In either situation, it is likely to stay a short time and will quickly move on if disturbed.

Meadow pipit

Anthus pratensis

14.5cm

J F M A M J
J A S O N D

Widespread, especially on heaths and moorland; also on downs, rough grassland and salt-marshes.

Fine bill

Slightly smaller, less elegant than tree pipit with plumper belly

White-sided tail

Flanks more streaked than tree pipit

Long hind claws

Brownish legs

PIED WAGTAIL

Young bird brownish-grey above, creamy below, with dark breast-band

NAMED FOR ITS PIED plumage and tail-wagging habit, this bird can be seen in towns and gardens, on farmland and often near water. Such places provide an abundance of the flies and other insects which form its diet. The pied wagtail is black above and white below, with a white face-patch and black chin and bib; the outer tail feathers are white. It has a shrill 'tchizzick' flight call. Cavities in cliffs, stream banks, walls and trees provide sites for its nest of vegetation lined with hair, wool or feathers. A mainland European race, seen in Britain on migration and known as the white wagtail, has pale grey upperparts and rump.

GARDEN WATCHING

Few birds are so at home on tarmac and concrete as this one: it is commonly seen in car parks and on footpaths as well as around park and garden ponds. It picks insects from the ground but also calls loudly from rooftops.

Pied wagtail

Motacilla alba yarrellii

18cm

J F M A M J
J A S O N D

Widespread in many open habitats. Some migrate to Continent in winter.

Male, summer
Female has dark grey back with
less black on hind crown and breast
(and in winter crown all-grey)

*Black cap
and bib
merge
in one*

*Long wagging
tail, with white
outer feathers*

White wagtail
Motacilla alba alba

*Pale grey
upper
body*

GREY WAGTAIL

A WALK BESIDE one of the rushing, tumbling streams in Britain's hill country may afford a glimpse of this elegant little bird. It spends much of its time walking along the water's edge or perching on a boulder, twitching its long tail as it watches for insects. It occasionally comes to garden ponds. The nest is always by fast-flowing water and usually in a crevice or hollow. The usual call is a loud, sharp 'tswick', which is shorter than the pied wagtail's.

Birds roost together in winter

Young bird yellow under tail, unlike young yellow wagtail

Grey wagtail

Motacilla cinerea

18cm

J F M A M J
J A S O N D

Widespread, but most abundant in northern and western uplands.

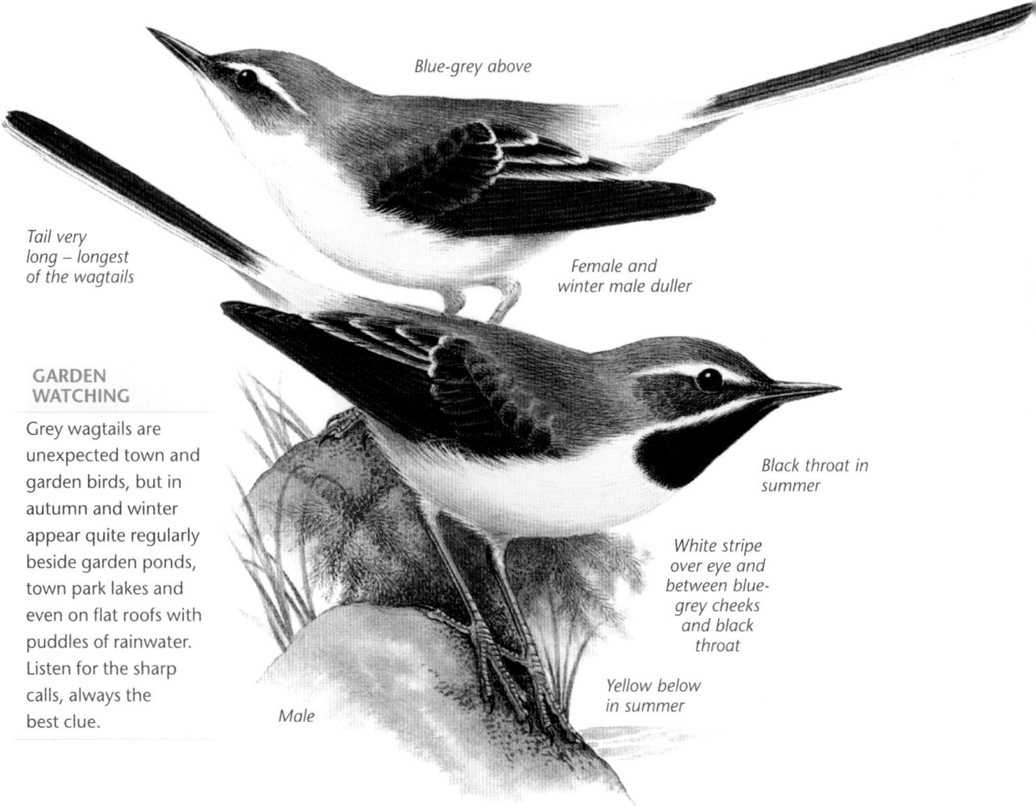

Blue-grey above

Tail very long – longest of the wagtails

Female and winter male duller

GARDEN WATCHING

Grey wagtails are unexpected town and garden birds, but in autumn and winter appear quite regularly beside garden ponds, town park lakes and even on flat roofs with puddles of rainwater. Listen for the sharp calls, always the best clue.

Black throat in summer

White stripe over eye and between blue-grey cheeks and black throat

Yellow below in summer

Male

WREN

TINY AND INCONSPICUOUS, even in a small garden, the wren can most easily be located by its voice, which is so loud for such a little bird. An explosive 'tit-tit-tit' is the call; the song is a loud, shrill, rattling warble. The male builds a number of domed nests, one of which the female chooses and lines with feathers. With a diet of small insects and spiders, it is hard hit by severe winters but, being a prolific breeder, it can soon make good losses of up to 80 per cent in a particularly hard winter. They may huddle together in communal roosts in cold weather.

Call is often made from a wall or shrub

Wren briefly glimpsed flitting between patches of undergrowth

Fast, straight, whirring flight on short rounded wings

Wren

Troglodytes troglodytes

9.5cm

J F M A M J
J A S O N D

In most habitats throughout Britain and Ireland, from city centres to remote islands.

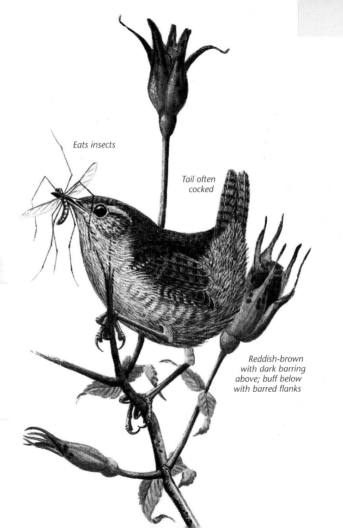

Eats insects

Tail often cocked

GARDEN WATCHING

Typically a bird of dark, dank, untidy places, the wren searches for insects behind garden sheds, amongst piles of pots and bits of timber, or in the tangled bottoms of hedges and flowerbeds.

Reddish-brown with dark barring above; buff below with barred flanks

DUNNOCK

THE DUNNOCK uses its wings in a curious display. A pair or even a small party of birds will perch in the open and wave their wings at each other in a sort of semaphore – this is an aggressive display during territorial disputes, often seen in gardens. The dunnock has long been called the hedge sparrow, but it is not a member of the sparrow family. It is identified by its grey head and underparts and thin bill. Its song is a jingling warble, rather like the wren's but less aggressive in tone. It lines its cup-shaped nest with hair and feathers.

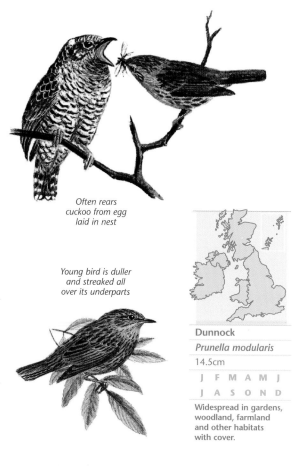

Often rears cuckoo from egg laid in nest

Young bird is duller and streaked all over its underparts

GARDEN WATCHING

A classic garden bird, the dunnock sings from hedgerows all summer and feeds on the ground beneath, or around the flowerbeds, with its characteristic slow, crouched, shuffling action. Watch for dunnocks waving their wings in territorial displays.

Dunnock

Prunella modularis

14.5cm

J F M A M J
J A S O N D

Widespread in gardens, woodland, farmland and other habitats with cover.

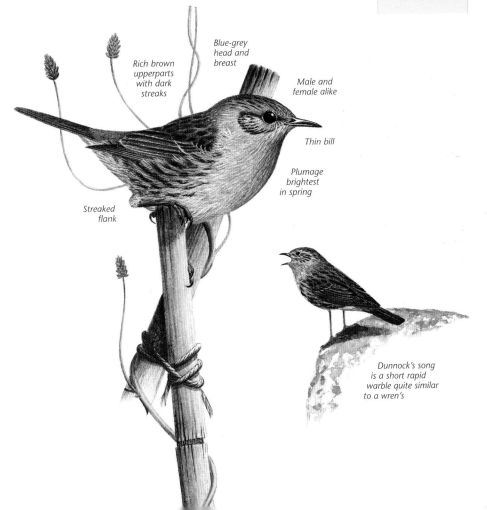

Rich brown
upperparts
with dark
streaks

Blue-grey
head and
breast

Male and
female alike

Thin bill

Plumage
brightest
in spring

Streaked
flank

Dunnock's song
is a short rapid
warble quite similar
to a wren's

ROBIN

THE ROBIN'S ASSOCIATION with
Christmas is appropriate, for it is
during winter that its colours are most
marked, with its breast at its reddest
and its back a warm brown, both
contrasting with whitish underparts.
Young birds have speckled plumage
with no red at first, often seen in
gardens in summer. The bird is tame
in town and city gardens, and often
accompanies gardeners to search for
insects and worms as the ground is dug
over. Away from habitation, it is shy
and retiring, inhabiting woodland and
hedges. Males are aggressive and guard
their territory possessively. The song
is a high, pleasant warble and the
loud alarm call a penetrating 'tic-tic'.

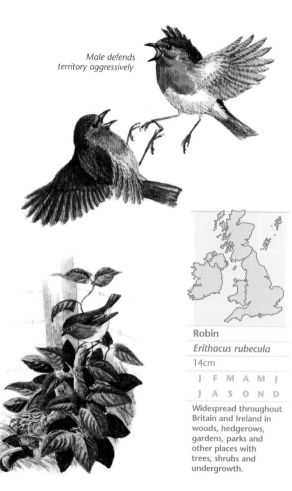

*Male defends
territory aggressively*

*Nest built in any
convenient container
such as an old teapot*

Robin

Erithacus rubecula

14cm

J F M A M J
J A S O N D

**Widespread throughout
Britain and Ireland in
woods, hedgerows,
gardens, parks and
other places with
trees, shrubs and
undergrowth.**

Song is thinner
and more
melancholy
after moulting
in autumn

Male and female
look the same

GARDEN WATCHING

Territorial all year, robins tend to be loners except when rearing their young. Only in hard winter weather will two sometimes share space more amicably on a bird table. Spring fights can be tempestuous affairs.

Whitish belly

Red breast, with pale blue-grey border separating it from olive-brown upperparts

NIGHTINGALE

THE MOST FAMOUS songster of all, the nightingale is a shy bird more often heard than seen and rare in British gardens. Renowned for singing at night, it can also be heard by day. The rich song has short phrases, single notes and harsh trills. It is far louder, richer and very different from that of the robin, although often confused with it, since that species also often sings by night. Nightingales live in coppiced woodland, thick hedges, bramble thickets and other areas with dense cover.

Chestnut tail and rump, conspicuous in flight

Juveniles heavily spotted and mottled; differs from young robin in having longer rufous tail

GARDEN WATCHING

The finest singer in all Europe, the nightingale is more likely in a garden in southern Europe than in England, where it prefers woodland thickets. It may sing from dense thickets around town parks: the song is best heard at dawn or dusk.

Nightingale

Luscinia megarhynchos

16.5cm

| | | | A | M | J |
| J | A | S | | | |

In wooded or scrubby habitats in England with dense cover, often near water; mainly in south and east.

Large dark eye, with pale ring

Buff underparts

Longish tail, reddish-brown

Male and female look the same

REDSTART

A FLASH OF BRIGHT, rusty red, low down in a tree or bush, reveals the redstart as it 'shimmers' its tail. This flickering motion plays an important part in courtship. A summer visitor from northern Africa, the male has a blue-grey back, black face and throat, white forehead, reddish breast and rusty rump and tail. The female is brown above and paler below, but has a rusty rump and tail like the male. The call is loud 'hooeeet-tac'; the song is a brief warble ending with a jingling rattle. The nest is in a crevice or hole in a wall or tree or in a nest box, but not often in gardens.

Female in flight

Female brown above and paler below

Redstart

Phoenicurus phoenicurus

14cm

J F M **A M J**
J A S O N D

Widespread in British woods and parkland; mainly in northern and western uplands (most numerous in Wales); rare in Ireland.

Blue-grey
back

Male,
summer

Black
mask

Reddish
breast

Rusty tail

**GARDEN & PARK
WATCHING**

A woodland bird, the
redstart turns up in
some unexpected
places while on
its autumn
migrations. It is a
good find in a garden
or town park, liable
to stay for a few
hours and then
be on its way.

Young is mottled, like young
robin, but with a rufous tail

BLACK REDSTART

THE BLACK REDSTART population in Britain began to grow during the Second World War, when bombed and derelict buildings and old docks made ideal nesting sites. Even today, fewer than 100 pairs breed in Britain, on sites that include factories, power stations and railway yards. They are town, rather than garden, birds. Males are sooty black above, females browner. The song is a loud, reedy warble. The birds usually nest on a ledge or crevice.

Migrant birds often seen on rocky beaches

Whitish wing-patches show as bird hovers

GARDEN WATCHING

Black redstarts are rare birds of towns and industrial sites in summer, but more widespread in winter when a few turn up in quarries and on rough, coastal ground, from which they may visit nearby gardens and buildings from time to time.

Juvenile is faintly barred and spotted, otherwise like female

Black redstart

Phoenicurus ochruros

14cm

| J | F | M | A | M | J |
| J | A | S | O | N | D |

Most nest on buildings, a few on cliffs and quarries; mainly in south-east England and Midlands; up to 50 or so in winter.

Male,
summer

Sooty black
upper body

White
wing-
patch

Female

No wing-
patch

Rusty red sides to tail
in male and female

Greyer than redstart

NA

STONECHAT

PERCHING ON A HIGH vantage point, the little, plump-bodied stonechat scolds intruders with its alarm call, a hard 'wee-tac-tac', like two pebbles being knocked together – hence the bird's name. It will only come to gardens that open onto heaths. It has a diet of insects, worms, spiders and some seeds and blackberries. This enables it to rear up to three, or even four, broods a year. The male has a black head, white half-collar, white patches on the wings and rump, and an orange-red breast. A nest of moss, grass and hair is well concealed, low in a bush.

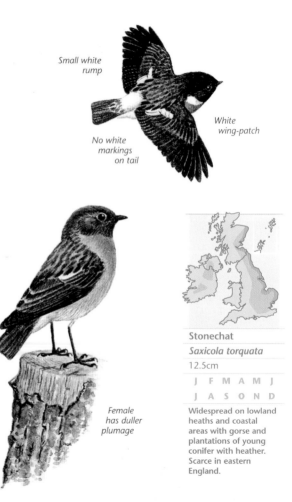

Small white rump

No white markings on tail

White wing-patch

Female has duller plumage

Stonechat

Saxicola torquata

12.5cm

J F M A M J
J A S O N D

Widespread on lowland heaths and coastal areas with gorse and plantations of young conifer with heather. Scarce in eastern England.

Black head

White half-collar

Male, summer

GARDEN WATCHING

Rough, bushy areas with heather, grass and ideally clumps of gorse attract stonechats, so only the larger, wilder town parks will normally see one in autumn or winter, when they wander a little from their usual breeding areas.

SONG THRUSH

BROKEN SNAIL SHELLS littering the ground around a large stone indicate the presence of the song thrush in the garden. Tapping noises may be the sound made by the bird as it smashes open the snails on a favourite 'anvil' to get at the contents. Aptly named, the bird is noted for its loud, rich song, which consists of a series of repeated musical phrases together lasting for 5 minutes or more. This impressive aria is usually delivered from a high perch. The bird's call is a thin 'sipp' in flight or a 'tchuck-tchuck' alarm note. It feeds mainly on snails, worms, insects and berries. There has been a 50 per cent decline in numbers between 1970 and 2001, with only a slight recent recovery.

Redwing

Golden-buff underwing distinguishes song thrush from redwing but hard to see

Song thrush

GARDEN WATCHING

In gardens the song thrush competes with blackbirds for worms, but has a special taste for snails, which it smashes noisily against a stone or paving slab, leaving small piles of broken shells on its regular 'anvil'.

Song thrush

Turdus philomelos

23cm

J F M A M J
J A S O N D

Widespread in woods, hedgerows, gardens and other areas with trees and shrubs for nesting. Passage migrants and winter visitors from Continent.

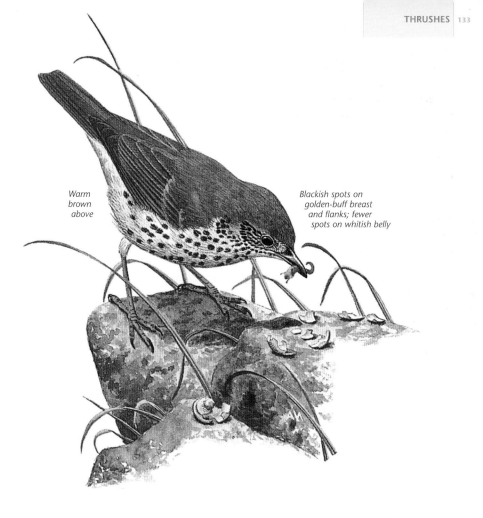

Warm
brown
above

Blackish spots on
golden-buff breast
and flanks; fewer
spots on whitish belly

MISTLE THRUSH

THE LARGEST OF THE British thrushes
is also the most boldly marked, with
bigger and blacker spots than those
of the song thrush. In flight, its white
underwing and white tips to the tail
help to distinguish it from other
thrushes. The call is a harsh, rattling
chatter and the song is a prolonged
series of short, repeated phrases and
fluty notes of considerable carrying
power. This is usually sung from the
top of high trees in wooded parks and
gardens, and can be heard throughout
winter as well as in spring and summer.
Mistle thrushes feed on berries
(including mistletoe), slugs, snails,
worms and insects. After the breeding
season small family groups often
feed together.

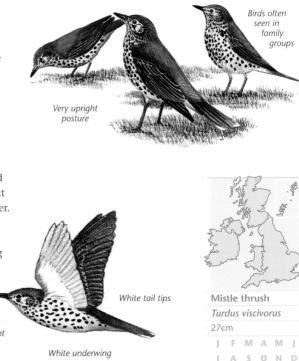

Birds often
seen in
family
groups

Very upright
posture

White tail tips

Dry, rattling
calls in flight

White underwing

Mistle thrush

Turdus viscivorus

27cm

J F M A M J
J A S O N D

Widespread in open
woods and other
areas with tall trees for
nesting and song-posts
and open ground for
feeding.

Grey-brown
above

Streaks on
wings

**GARDEN
WATCHING**

The biggest thrush,
this is a bird of large,
open parks and big
gardens with tall trees:
it is not often seen
on smaller lawns in
enclosed spaces. If
disturbed, it is likely
to fly off high and fast
above the trees: the
smaller song thrush
dashes into the
nearest hedge.

Large, bold
spots on
whitish
underparts

Longer wings
and tail than
song thrush

BLACKBIRD

THE BLACKBIRD'S RICH, fluty, warbling song, punctuated by pauses, is a herald of spring in any garden, and its alarm call of 'pink-pink-pink' is also a familiar sound. The male is distinguished by its all-black plumage, rich egg-yellow bill and eye-ring, while females are brown, with mottled underparts. The blackbird's diet consists of insects, berries and worms, and it can often be seen standing on the lawn with head cocked to one side, listening and looking for worms before pulling them out of the ground.

Blackbirds feed with migrant thrushes, such as redwings

Female is brown, with blurred spots on underparts

Blackbird

Turdus merula

25cm

| J | F | M | A | M | J |
| J | A | S | O | N | D |

Widespread in Britain and Ireland; Continental visitors in winter.

Juvenile is similar to female but has pale spots on upperparts

Orange-yellow bill and eye-ring

All-black plumage

Male

GARDEN WATCHING

This is the finest garden songster, a common bird anywhere where there are trees, shrubs and lawns, over which it searches diligently for worms. It is a regular visitor to bird tables but prefers feeding on the ground beneath.

FIELDFARE

*Orange-buff breast
heavily speckled*

*Black tail contrasts with
grey rump in flight*

AUTUMN AND WINTER sees large flocks
of these colourful thrushes arriving
in the British Isles from Scandinavia
and Finland. The birds' 'chack-chack'
chattering calls can be heard as they
fly onto fields to feed on worms and
insects. Noisy scuffles are common
among flocks of fieldfares as they
feed, and berry-bearing bushes are
defended against all-comers. Later
in winter, when the berry stocks have
been eaten by thrushes and other
birds, fieldfares, along with their
relatives, visit gardens to gorge
on fallen apples.

*Noisy scuffles
common as
birds feed*

Fieldfare

Turdus pilaris

25cm

J F M A M
O N D

Feeds in fields with
short grass, arable
crops or soil, also in
hedgerows, gardens
and orchards; very few
breed in Scotland and
northern England, but
many visit the British
Isles in winter.

Bold white underwing

Grey rump

Chestnut back

Grey head and nape

Black tail and flight feathers

GARDEN WATCHING

Hard winter weather drives fieldfares into gardens in search of food, especially berries and fallen apples. They may squabble with the local blackbirds and song thrushes, competing with them for precious food resources in difficult times.

REDWING

LEAVING ITS MAINLAND European breeding grounds in autumn, the redwing is a passage migrant and winter visitor to the British Isles, although a very few pairs breed in Scotland. In September and October flocks can be heard flying over, uttering their thin 'seeip' contact call. The adults are smaller and darker than the song thrush, brown above, with a pale streak above the eye. Below they are whitish, with a yellowish-buff tinge to the breast, marked with dark spots and streaks, and have reddish flanks and under-wing patches. Their favoured food is hawthorn, holly and other berries. Worms, snails and insects are also eaten.They come to gardens mainly in severe weather.

Redwings often feed with other thrushes

GARDEN WATCHING

This is a small, dark, neat thrush, a winter bird in Britain, which comes to gardens mainly in severe weather. It joins other thrushes, feeding on berries and the remains of fallen apples: such food is often a life saver.

Redwing

Turdus iliacus

21cm

J	F	M	A	M	J
J	A	S	O	N	D

Feeds on fields with short grass or crops, or soil and in hedgerows, gardens and orchards.

Rusty-red underwing
patches

Dark brown
upperparts

Pale line
over eye

Rust-red
flanks

BLACKCAP

IN RECENT YEARS some blackcaps have started braving the English winter, visiting bird tables and gardens for food, but they are normally summer visitors from the Mediterranean, with smaller numbers wintering in Africa. They have a rich, warbling song, shorter and more variable than that of the garden warbler. The male's black cap distinguishes it from all other British warblers. Insects are its main food.

GARDEN & PARK WATCHING

This is a parkland bird, also found in larger areas of wooded gardens, or in thickets of rhododendrons and other shrubs between scattered trees. Listen for its magnificent song and look for it at the bird table in winter, too.

Young all have brown caps

Grey-brown back

Courting male raises feathers, droops wings and spreads tail

Blackcap

Sylvia atricapilla

14cm

| | | M | A | M | J |
| J | A | S | O | | |

Woodlands, hedgerows, scrub; some in parks and gardens. Widespread, except in northern Scotland and northern half of western Ireland.

Black cap

Male has greyish-brown upperparts; female is browner above

Rusty brown cap

Grey below

Female

Male

Brownish-grey below

GARDEN WARBLER

DESPITE ITS NAME, the garden warbler is found only in large, mature gardens with trees and shrubs. It is more a bird of open woodland and copses, where it announces its presence by its melodic song or harsh 'tacc-tacc' and grating 'churr' calls. In appearance it is a rather heavy-looking, short-billed bird, with no distinctive features. Before migrating back to Africa in winter it fattens up on berries.

Tail spread and wings fluttered in courtship display

Nest built low, often in brambles

Garden warbler

Sylvia borin

14cm

| | | | A | M | J |
| J | A | S | O | | |

Woods and bushy areas, especially in coppice and thickets. Not in much of northern Scotland and Ireland.

Olive-grey-brown
upper parts

Short bill

Plain
face

**GARDEN
WATCHING**

Names can be
misleading. This is not
a common garden
bird, but you might
see one or two in the
early autumn, feeding
on elderberries or
honeysuckle berries,
fattening up before
the long migration
flight south.

Pale buff
underparts

Male and female
look the same

WHITETHROAT

ONCE THE COMMONEST warbler to be found in Britain, the whitethroat suffered a severe fall in numbers between the autumn of 1968 and the spring of 1969, because of a severe drought south of the Sahara, where the birds winter. Since then the breeding population has fluctuated at around a million pairs. The whitethroat's song, a short, scratchy warble, is often uttered by the male in a brief dancing display flight. Whitethroats like nettles and brambles and are not very common in gardens.

White outer tail feathers

GARDEN WATCHING

Brambles, thorn bushes and rough hedgerows beside large gardens may be good places for spotting whitethroats; otherwise they are rather sparse visitors while on migration in spring and autumn. Look for the reddish-brown wing patches.

Whitethroat

Sylvia communis

14cm

J	F	M	A	M	J
J	A	S	O	N	D

Widespread in scrub, dense hedges, and other places with thick vegetation, except in Scottish Highlands.

Female

Brownish head; crown often peaked

Grey head

Long tail is edged with white

White throat

Male

Reddish-brown wings

Pale legs

LESSER WHITETHROAT

ONLY MARGINALLY SMALLER than the whitethroat, the lesser whitethroat prefers areas with taller trees and shrubs and dense cover, especially bramble, blackthorn or hawthorn hedges or thickets. It is distinguished by its more uniform brown wings, which lack the contrasting reddish tinge of the whitethroat's wings. The bird's song often starts with a low warble, then continues with a rattling note repeated five or six times, audible at some distance.

Shyer than the whitethroat, usually concealed in foliage

The song is often delivered from the shelter of a bush or thicket.

Lesser whitethroat

Sylvia curruca

13.5cm

| J | F | M | A | M | J |
| J | A | S | O | N | D |

Rarely breeds in most of Scotland or Ireland; may be declining.

Greyish upperparts

Dark cheeks

White throat

Dark cheek (variable) and dull brown wings

Tail rather shorter than whitethroat's, but also has white outer feathers

GARDEN WATCHING

This small, neat warbler likes dense thickets and tall, old, dark hedges of blackthorn and maple; in autumn, however, they come to gardens to feed on berries of elder or honeysuckle, often giving close views.

Underparts pale buff or have pinkish tinge

Dark legs

WILLOW WARBLER

BY FAR THE COMMONEST of all warblers in the British Isles, the willow warbler is a summer visitor from Africa. Some 3 million pairs inhabit open woodland and bushy places – for the bird is in no way confined to willows – though it is not common in gardens. Its song, a wistful cadence of soft, liquid notes that descend in a pitch and end in a flourish, can be heard all summer as the bird darts restlessly among the foliage, feeding on its insect prey. Unusually, the willow warbler moults completely, replacing all its plumage twice a year.

Courting male fans out tail and makes wings quiver

Young birds more yellow

Willow warbler

Phylloscopus trochilus

11.5cm

| | | | A | M | J |
| J | A | S | | | |

Widespread in woods and scrub.

GARDEN & PARK WATCHING

This declining summer warbler is sometimes seen briefly in gardens but more often on the bushy edges of parks, rather than in the neater, well-kept parts. It prefers tall willows and birches, or lightly wooded areas.

Flight fast and agile

Greenish or olive above

Larger than chiffchaff with more noticeable pale streak above eye

Yellowish below

Legs usually pale

CHIFFCHAFF

Parent alights above
nest and slips down
through foliage

THE CHIFFCHAFF is extremely similar in appearance to the willow warbler and can most readily be identified by its distinctive eponymous song. It consists of a prolonged repetition of 'chiff and chaff' notes, the first higher pitched than the second, in varying order, such as 'chiff-chaff-chiff-chaff-chiff-chiff-chaff-chaff-chiff-chaff . . .'. Its call is a clear 'hooit', shorter, less disyllabic and with the emphasis on the second higher syllable than the willow warbler's call. Closely observed, the chiffchaff is dumpier and more rounded than the willow warbler, and slightly duller, more greyish-green in colour above and paler yellow below, with less pronounced pale streaks above the eyes. Dark legs are another distinction. Young chiffchaffs are much yellower than adults and even more like willow warblers though usually rather duller.

Courting male
'floats' down
on spread wings

Chiffchaff

Phylloscopus collybita

11.5cm

J F M A M J

J A S O N D

Wood and scrub with trees (though not usually conifers); some visit gardens in winter

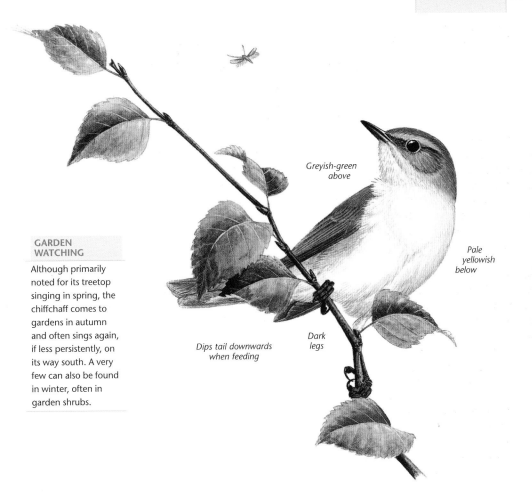

Greyish-green
above

Pale
*yellowish
below*

**GARDEN
WATCHING**

Although primarily
noted for its treetop
singing in spring, the
chiffchaff comes to
gardens in autumn
and often sings again,
if less persistently, on
its way south. A very
few can also be found
in winter, often in
garden shrubs.

*Dips tail downwards
when feeding*

*Dark
legs*

GOLDCREST

THIS IS THE SMALLEST BIRD in Europe. Although often allowing a close approach, it spends most of its time flitting from branch to branch in the top of coniferous trees, seeking the spiders, insects and larvae which form its diet. The bright orange centre to the crown of the male is visible only at close range; the female lacks the orange feathers to her all-yellow crest. A thin, blackish 'moustache' at the sides of the bill tends to give the goldcrest a mournful appearance. Juveniles lack the coloured crest, being dull greenish above and pale below.

Nest usually built in conifer

GARDEN WATCHING

Few birds pay so little attention to people as the goldcrest, which, so long as it is not pushed too closely, simply gets on with its job of searching for insects and spiders. It is most often found where there are coniferous trees.

Goldcrest

Regulus regulus

9cm

J F M A M J
J A S O N D

Most are in coniferous woodland, but also breeds in churchyard yews, parks and large gardens.

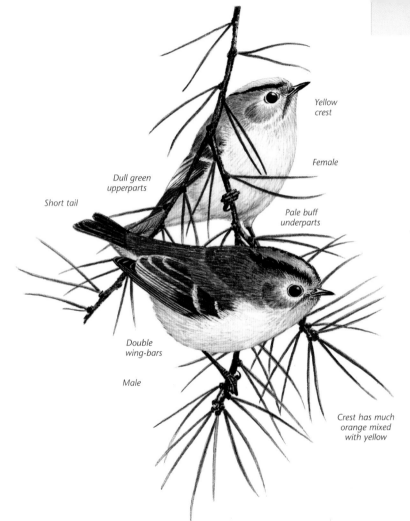

Yellow
crest

Female

Dull green
upperparts

Short tail

Pale buff
underparts

Double
wing-bars

Male

Crest has much
orange mixed
with yellow

FIRECREST

SIMILAR IN APPEARANCE to the
goldcrest – and only fractionally larger
– the firecrest is much less commonly
seen, being mainly a passage migrant
in autumn and spring. It can be
distinguished from the goldcrest by
the black and white eye-stripes in both
adults and juveniles and, in the adult
male, far more orange in the more
sharply black-bordered crest. Some
females also have a little orange in the
crown. Adult firecrests are a brighter
green on the back and whiter below
than goldcrests, and have bronze-
coloured patches on the shoulders,
especially in the male.

Black and
white eye-stripe

Courting
male raises
crest

GARDEN
WATCHING

Very like a goldcrest, with more colour and
pattern around the head and neck, this is a
much rarer bird, usually associated with holly
and conifers, or in low, dense thickets in
autumn and winter.

Firecrest

Regulus ignicapillus

9cm

| J | F | M | A | M | J |
| J | A | S | O | N | D |

Scarce breeder in
woods and regular
passage migrant in
southern Britain; some
winter in scrub in
south-west England.

Juvenile
lacks crest

Mainly fiery
orange crest

Male

Bronze
shoulder-
patches

Whitish underparts have
shining 'silky' appearance

SPOTTED FLYCATCHER

SITTING ON A LOW branch or other perch, the spotted flycatcher watches for its flying insect prey. Periodically it darts out and catches flies and other insects with an audible snap of its broad-based bill and quickly returns to its perch. The bird's plumage is mainly grey-brown above, pale below. Arriving from Africa in May, the birds seek out woodland edges and glades, gardens, parks and heathland. Both birds build a cup-shaped nest of dried grass and lichen among creepers such as ivy on walls or fences, in old nests of other birds or in an open-fronted nest box. Calls are a squeaky 'tzee' and a sharp 'tzee-chick' of alarm, its simple song a series of quiet squeaky and scratch warbling notes, well spaced out.

Juveniles prominently spotted and scaly

Spotted flycatcher

Muscicapa striata

14cm

Widespread, open wooded areas, large mature gardens, parks; numbers decreasing.

Broad-based flat bill makes audible snap when bird flies out to catch insects

Soft, blurred streaks on breast and head

Very short legs; upright pose

Grey-brown upperparts, silvery-whitish-buff below with pale edges to wing feathers

Male and female look alike

GARDEN & PARK WATCHING

Although declining, the spotted flycatcher remains a typical bird of gardens and small parks, often nesting in creepers or even hanging baskets. It sits on a prominent perch and flies out to snatch an insect and back again.

PIED FLYCATCHER

NORMALLY BREEDING in holes in trees, this summer-visiting migrant from Africa has spread in Britain with the encouragement of nest boxes deliberately placed for them in woodland in areas where natural tree holes are in short supply. Despite this, the species appears to have declined here over the past century. The male in his smart breeding plumage is black above and white below, with a large white wing-patch and white forehead; the female lacks the white forehead and is brown above. The birds catch insects in flight but unlike spotted flycatchers, rarely return to the same perch and also snatch prey such as caterpillars from leaves or even the ground. Calls are a sharp 'whit' and a 'tic' and the song a simple sweet warbling with marked changes of pitch.

Catches more insects on the ground than the spotted flycatcher

Female brown above, without white forehead

Pied flycatcher

Ficedula hypoleuca

12.5cm

| | | | A | M | J |
| J | A | S | O | | |

Breeds in mature deciduous woodland, especially oak, mainly in western Britain; most abundant in Wales; elsewhere a regular passage migrant.

White forehead

Mainly black above

White breast

Male

Large white wing-patch

GARDEN WATCHING

Only if you live close to a deciduous wood are you likely to see pied flycatchers in summer; you might even attract a pair to a nest box. In autumn, you may have a better chance of a brief visit from a passing migrant.

LONG-TAILED TIT

THE TAIL OF THIS tiny bird is more than half its total length and conspicuous, especially in flight. The birds are almost always on the move in woods, commons, wasteland and hedges, feeding on small insects and spiders, as well as some seeds. Severe winters take their toll, and in some years reduce the bird's population by 80 per cent. The deep, purse-shaped nest is a masterpiece in moss, bound together with cobwebs and hair and camouflaged on the outside with lichen and lined with many hundreds of feathers.

Birds roam about in small groups

Parents feeding a brood of young are often aided by one or more unpaired adults

GARDEN WATCHING

If you see one, you will usually see several of these tiny birds, which go around in little gangs of half a dozen or so, sometimes more, and flit from tree to tree one after the other. They are increasingly noted on hanging feeders in gardens.

Long-tailed tit

Aegithalos caudatus

14cm

J F M A M J

J A S O N D

Widespread, but more abundant in the south.

Long tail conspicuous in flight

Round head and tiny round body

Very long black tail has white outer feathers

Head mainly blackish

Juvenile duller, with shorter tail

Flight undulating on whirring wings with tail moving

White crown

Tiny, stubby bill

Roosting birds huddle in tightly packed clumps for warmth

Pink flanks and broad pink bar on shoulder

Black band above eye

BLUE TIT

FOR MANY PEOPLE the blue tit is the star performer in the garden bird show, combining the talents of acrobat, conjurer and songster. It is small and highly adaptable: it was the blue tit that first cracked the problem of how to pierce milk-bottle tops to reach the layer of cream at the top – a practice that has almost vanished due to the popularity of semi-skimmed milk and decline in doorstep deliveries. Blue tits cannot digest lactose in milk, but cream presents no such problem. Originally a woodland bird, the blue tit will nest wherever there is a suitable small hole in a tree or a nesting-box. It has a large vocabulary of calls and a song comprising of two or three thin, high notes followed by a rapid trill.

Young birds are duller with greenish caps and yellow faces

Birds readily use nest-boxes with a small entrance hole about 30mm across

Blue tit

Parus caeruleus

11.5cm

J F M A M J
J A S O N D

Woods (largest populations in deciduous woods, especially oak), parks and gardens in all areas, including cities.

Blue cap

Green back

White face with black eye-stripe

Yellow underparts

Bluish wings and tail with white wing-bar

GARDEN WATCHING

No bird is so closely associated with bird feeders as the blue tit; in gardens it is often tempted to use a nest box, but the abundance of caterpillars found in spring in a wood is rarely found in a garden, and garden blue tits rear far fewer young.

GREAT TIT

THE GREAT TIT is the biggest, brightest and noisiest member of the tit family in the British Isles. Experts have identified over 50 distinct calls and songs, including the scolding 'cha-cha-cha', the chaffinch-like 'chink' calls and the often-heard, loud 'teacher, teacher, teacher' song and its variants. It is also extremely adept at finding ways to reach tempting morsels of food, such as a nut at the end of a piece of string. Its nest is usually in a hole in a tree or a wall, or in a nest box, but occasional sites include, letter boxes and drainpipes.

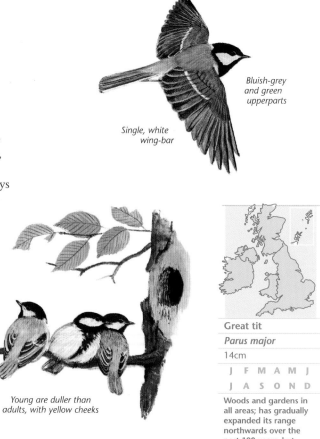

Bluish-grey and green upperparts

Single, white wing-bar

Young are duller than adults, with yellow cheeks

Great tit

Parus major

14cm

J F M A M J
J A S O N D

Woods and gardens in all areas; has gradually expanded its range northwards over the past 100 years, but does not occur in Orkney or Shetland.

Black and white head

Compared with the blue tit, this is a more substantial bird, and something of a bully at the bird feeder: but it is just trying its best to survive. It deserves our support, as it is such a handsome creature, with a cheery, simple song in early spring.

Male

Yellow belly, black stripe down body; wider and glossier in males

White outer tail feathers

COAL TIT

THE SMALLEST BRITISH TIT, the coal tit's favourite habitat is coniferous woodland, where its high-pitched 'tsee' call and sweet piping 'wee-choo, wee-choo' song (with the accent on the first syllable) can be heard. It often visits bird tables, especially for nuts, meat and suet scraps and tends to fly off with them to hide and eat later. It survives prolonged periods of snow by feeding on insects living or sheltering beneath the bark of trees.

Coal tits eat insects under tree bark

GARDEN WATCHING

Coal tits love peanuts and sunflower seeds: they take them away to feed in a quieter spot, or to hide them ready to eat later. Even against a blue tit they look tiny and only the goldcrest is smaller than this smart little bird.

Young have yellow cheeks and nape-patches

Coal tit

Parus ater

11.5cm

J F M A M J
J A S O N D

Widespread in woods, especially conifers but also in mixed and deciduous woods, also in gardens.

Black cap

White patch on
back of head

Olive-grey
upperparts

White
cheek

Buff underparts

Two white
wing-bars

MARSH TIT

Feeds mainly on lower vegetation; quite often with other tit species in mixed roving flocks in winter

IN SPITE OF ITS NAME, the marsh tit is rarely found in marshland but favours woods, heaths and hedges. It is almost indistinguishable from the willow tit at a distance except by its call and song. Its calls include a distinctive, loud, explosive 'pitchew' or a scolding 'chickabee-bee-bee-bee'. The song is a single, repeated ringing liquid 'chip, chip, chip'. Closely observed, its black crown is glossy and it lacks the pale wing-patch of the willow tit (see page 173).

Unlike willow tit, no pale wing-patch

Marsh tit

Parus palustris

11.5cm

J F M A M J
J A S O N D

Deciduous woods in England and Wales, visits gardens, especially in winter. Rare in Scotland and not in Ireland.

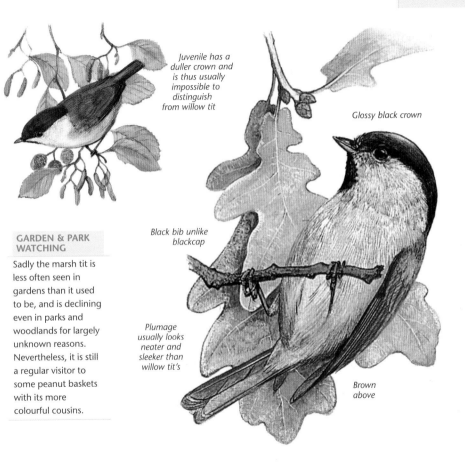

Juvenile has a duller crown and is thus usually impossible to distinguish from willow tit

Glossy black crown

Black bib unlike blackcap

Plumage usually looks neater and sleeker than willow tit's

Brown above

GARDEN & PARK WATCHING

Sadly the marsh tit is less often seen in gardens than it used to be, and is declining even in parks and woodlands for largely unknown reasons. Nevertheless, it is still a regular visitor to some peanut baskets with its more colourful cousins.

WILLOW TIT

FOR YEARS THE willow tit was mistaken for the marsh tit, and it was not recognised as a separate species until 1897. Gradually it was realised that the willow tit is almost as common as the marsh tit. For unknown reasons, both species have declined in recent years. It is distinguished from the marsh tit by its matt black crown, less extensive white on cheeks, more diffuse black bib and pale panel on the wing. It can also be identified by its voice. The call is a loud, harsh 'tchay' (like a similar call of the marsh tit's) and a diagnostic, quiet buzzing 'zee-zee-zee'; the song is a short, rich, melodious warbling, unusual among tits.

Unlike the marsh tit, the bird excavates its nest-hole in a soft tree-trunk

GARDEN WATCHING

Having suffered a fast and severe decline, the willow tit is now scarce in gardens, where it needs to be distinguished from the very similar marsh tit: concentrate, if you can, on its calls. It typically takes a nut and quickly flies away with it.

Matt
black
crown

Black bib
unlike
blackcap

Pale
wing-patch

Like marsh tit, has brown
upperparts and buff underparts
with white on cheeks

Willow tit

Parus montanus

11.5cm

J F M A M J
J A S O N D

Damp woods, often
near rivers, streams or
flooded gravel pits and
reservoirs; less likely to
visit gardens than
marsh tit. Found in
England, Wales and
southern Scotland;
absent in Ireland.

NUTHATCH

THE NUTHATCH IS UNIQUE in its ability to move down a tree-trunk as easily as up it. It picks up insects from the bark, and also feeds on hazel and beech-nuts, acorns and seeds. The nuts are placed into a crack in the bark, and the bird hammers them open to reach the kernel. The nuthatch's call is a loud repeated 'chwit' or a rapid, trilling 'chirirliri'. Nuthatches breed in tree-holes or nest-boxes, making the entrance smaller by plastering round it with mud, which hardens in the sun.

Female uses mud to reduce size of nesting hole to prevent larger birds from taking it over

Tree is climbed (and descended) in zigzag hops

Nuthatch

Sitta europaea

14cm

J F M A M J
J A S O N D

Deciduous woods and mature gardens with trees in England and Wales; has recently started breeding in southern Scotland.

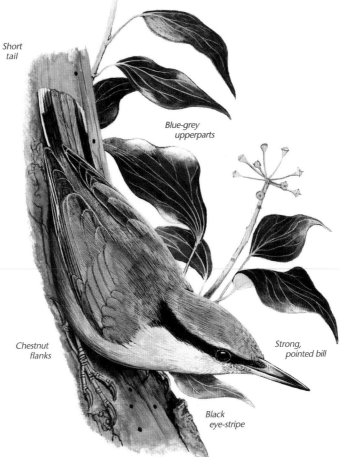

Short tail

Blue-grey upperparts

GARDEN & PARK WATCHING

Peanut and seed baskets attract nuthatches if the garden is close to a wood or parkland with tall, old trees. Nuthatches also feed on the ground beneath, taking spilled seeds, which they may wedge in a bark crevice and hammer noisily.

Chestnut flanks

Strong, pointed bill

Black eye-stripe

TREECREEPER

THANKS TO ITS LARGE, sharp claws and stiff, fairly long, frayed-looking tail, the little treecreeper can progress jerkily up tree-trunks in its search for bark-dwelling insects. It climbs spirally up one tree and then – because it cannot hop down like the nuthatch – flies down to the base of another and starts its upward journey again. The treecreeper's song, a trill followed by a warble, is thin and high-pitched, its call a shrill 'tseee'.
In winter, treecreepers and nuthatches associate with flocks of tits as they search for insects. The nest is usually behind loose bark or ivy on an old tree. The young climb well, but are poor fliers at first.

Pale band on wing

Pointed tips to tail

Treecreeper

Certhia familiaris

12.5cm

J F M A M J
J A S O N D

Woodlands in most parts of Britain and Ireland; also visits large gardens and hedgerows, especially in winter.

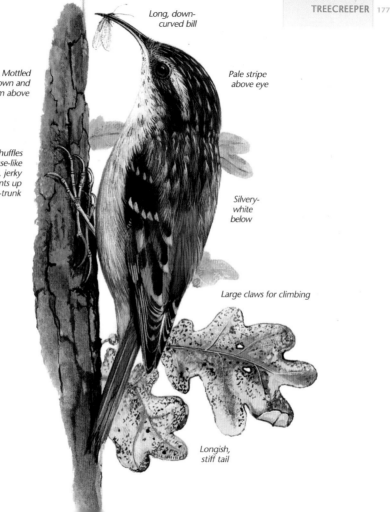

Long, down-
curved bill

Mottled
brown and
cream above

Pale stripe
above eye

Shuffles
mouse-like
with fast, jerky
movements up
tree-trunk

Silvery-
white
below

Large claws for climbing

Longish,
stiff tail

GARDEN WATCHING

It is a rare sight to see a treecreeper on a nut basket; usually, they are not much helped by artificial feeding in gardens, but simply choose to search the bark of garden trees for insects and spiders, and then move quietly on their way.

JAY

THE MOST COLOURFUL member of the crow family in the British Isles, the jay is heavily dependent on trees – especially oaks – and is more often heard than seen. It scolds woodland intruders with a loud, harsh 'skraaark'. When seen, the pinkish-buff plumage, streaked crown, white rump and blue wing-patch are distinctive. A major food is acorns, which are often collected and buried among fallen leaves and twigs to be eaten in the winter. Beech-nuts, peas, fruit and berries are similarly stored. Jays also eat small mammals, insects and worms, and will sometimes raid the nests of other birds for eggs or young.

Jay buries acorns and other food

Prominent white rump and wing-patches

Jay

Garrulus glandarius

34cm

J F M A M J
J A S O N D

Woodlands in most of the British Isles, but not in northern Scotland and part of western Ireland.

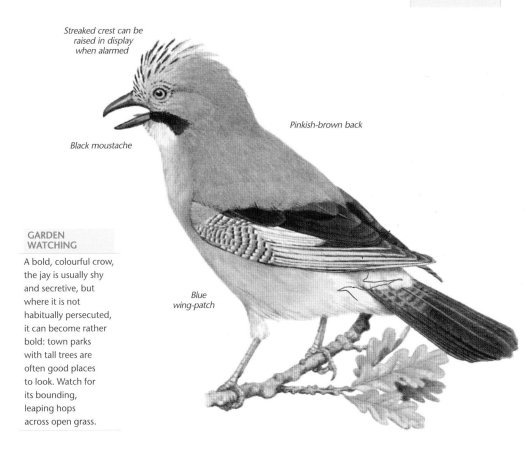

Streaked crest can be
raised in display
when alarmed

Pinkish-brown back

Black moustache

Blue
wing-patch

GARDEN WATCHING

A bold, colourful crow,
the jay is usually shy
and secretive, but
where it is not
habitually persecuted,
it can become rather
bold: town parks
with tall trees are
often good places
to look. Watch for
its bounding,
leaping hops
across open grass.

MAGPIE

ONCE HEAVILY persecuted and considered a pest, the magpie is now increasing in numbers, especially in suburban areas where it was once unknown. Its black and white plumage and long wedge-shaped black tail, with multicoloured iridescence in sunlight, make it one of the easiest of all birds to identify. During the nesting season magpies often stay hidden in overgrown hedgerows and thickets, their presence only revealed by their call, a hoarse, laughing chatter 'chacha-chacha-chak'. The birds build a large, domed nest of sticks. Young birds, which have shorter tails, leave the nest after three to four weeks. Though often accused of wiping out songbirds, detailed research shows that its habit of eating eggs and young has a negligible effect on their overall populations – indeed where magpies thrive, so do songbirds – and it has a wide diet, including berries, seeds and other plant material in winter, carion and insects, including many harmful to farming and gardening.

Magpies steal eggs and sometimes nestlings of other birds as part of a wide-ranging diet

Long tail

Tail tinged with purple, reddish, blue and green

Magpie

Pica pica

45cm

J F M A M J
J A S O N D

Widespread in many habitats, from farm-land, moorland and other open areas to city centres, as long as there are trees for roosting. Absent in northern Scotland.

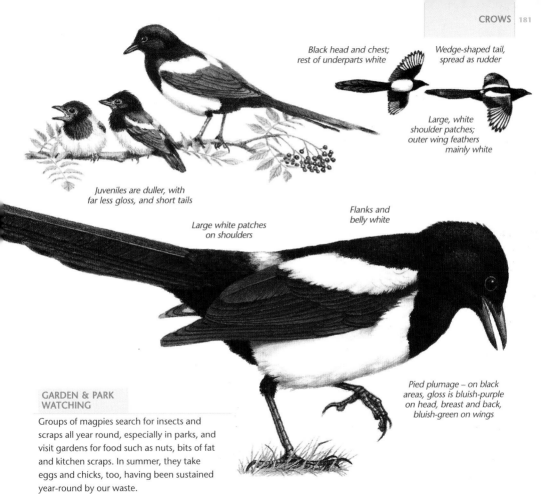

Black head and chest; rest of underparts white

Wedge-shaped tail, spread as rudder

Large, white shoulder patches; outer wing feathers mainly white

Juveniles are duller, with far less gloss, and short tails

Large white patches on shoulders

Flanks and belly white

Pied plumage – on black areas, gloss is bluish-purple on head, breast and back, bluish-green on wings

GARDEN & PARK WATCHING

Groups of magpies search for insects and scraps all year round, especially in parks, and visit gardens for food such as nuts, bits of fat and kitchen scraps. In summer, they take eggs and chicks, too, having been sustained year-round by our waste.

JACKDAW

EASILY IDENTIFIED by its grey nape, which contrasts with its darker grey and black plumage, jackdaws are very sociable and usually found in pairs or flocks. They often feed and roost with rooks. The bird's diet includes cereals, potatoes, fruit and berries as well as insects, mice and worms. Jackdaws often store and hide food and sometimes steal the eggs and nestlings of other birds. They nest in tree holes, old nests of other birds, rabbit burrows or chimney pots. The main call is a loud, explosive 'tchack' , a long 'kyaaar' and a shrill 'keeya'.

Faster wing-beats than rooks or crows

Short bill

Jackdaws flock together on derelict buildings such as castles

Jackdaw

Corvus monedula

33cm

J F M A M J
J A S O N D

Breed on cliffs, quarries, ruins, chimneypots and old woodlands through-out Britain and Ireland.

Whitish eyes

Grey nape

Black back

Dark grey underparts

Relatively short legs

GARDEN & PARK WATCHING

Tall chimneys are the best habitat for jackdaws, but they also nest in cavities in old, tall trees, so they can be seen around large houses and town gardens and in established parks. They come to the garden to feed, too, on insects and scraps.

ROOK

AS MANY AS 6000 rooks have been counted in one raucous rookery, their nests at the tops of tall trees standing out in springtime against a network of bare branches. They feed in flocks on roadside verges, rubbish tips and fields, especially on permanent pasture on farmland, where the soil contains many of the bird's favourite insect foods – leatherjackets and wireworms. A bare, white face-patch, elongated thigh feathers and highly glossy purplish-black plumage distinguish the adult rook from the similar but more solitary carrion crow. Juveniles lack the pale face-patch but have the adults' distinctive, slim, pointed bill shape.

Throat pouch distended when carrying food

Wedge-shaped tail

GARDEN & PARK WATCHING

Occasionally a rook will copy other birds and hang, clumsily, from a peanut basket, but usually they are not garden birds, but more likely in large town parks. They even feed around the car parks, searching for insects killed by traffic and scattered crumbs.

Rook

Corvus frugilegus

45cm

J F M A M J
J A S O N D

Widespread, especially in lowland farmland with tall trees for nesting. Absent only from treeless uplands and large towns.

Crown often
looks peaked

Black plumage with
strong purple gloss

Bare white
face-patch –
quite slender
pointed bill
with unfeathered
nostrils

Long thigh
feathers

Juvenile has dark
face and beak

CARRION CROW

SMALLER THAN THE RAVEN but far more common, the carrion crow has few friends. Its scavenging habits and harsh croaking call have not endeared it to man, and it has been persecuted because of its liking for grain and root crops and thieving of the eggs and chicks of game birds. Birds south and east of north-west Scotland are usually all black carrion crows, while more northerly very close relatives (formerly regarded as a subspecies of the carrion crow) have grey bodies and are known as hooded crows. In between, the two species often interbreed, producing hybrids that have black plumage with some grey markings.

Often feed on carrion

Square-ended tail

Grey body; black wings

Hooded crow
Corvus cornix

Carrion crow

Corvus corone

47cm

J F M A M J
J A S O N D

Widespread. Hooded crow in north-west Scotland and Ireland; carrion crow elsewhere; hybrids along zone of overlap.

Heavier, blunter bill than rook with feathered nostrils

Square-ended tail

GARDEN & PARK WATCHING

Crows will perch high on tall garden trees, such as big cedars and pines, calling loudly, and feed on nearby sports pitches and in parks so long as they are not disturbed. They are big, dramatic birds for such intimate locations.

All-black plumage is only slightly glossy

WAXWING

WINTER VISITORS to the British Isles, waxwings do not breed here; mostly only 100 or so are seen, but during 'interruption' years when their breeding populations in northern Scandinavia and Russia outstrip the food supplies, several thousands arrive here searching for berries – the rowan, hawthorn and whitebeam are favourites, though they also eat rose, cotoneaster, and many other berries and some seeds. Adults are pinkish-brown, darker on the back, with a unique long, pointed crest, a black mask and throat, grey rump and yellow-tipped black tail. Black, yellow and white appear in the wings with the red waxy-looking blobs that give the bird its name. The call is a shrill, trilling, bell-like 'sirrr'.

Flies swiftly and directly in flocks

Flight silhouette and alternate flapping and closed wing flight action resembles starlings, but waxwings have longer, plumper bodies and less dart-like flight

Waxwings gather in groups to eat berries from trees and shrubs

Waxwing

Bombycilla garrulus

18cm

J	F	M	A	M	J

J	A	S	O	N	D

Shrubs and trees, mainly in east; numerous only in occasional years.

Ponds and puddles are drinking places

Waxy red tips on wing feathers visible at close range

Crest

Black on throat and around eyes

GARDEN & PARK WATCHING

This is an exciting garden find: in some years small flocks reach the UK and are found wherever there are berries in gardens and parks, but in most years waxwings are scarce or absent: enjoy them when you can.

Dumpy body

Multi-coloured wings; dull reddy-brown under tail

Yellow tip to tail

STARLING

THIS ASSERTIVE and noisy bird is as familiar in towns as it is in the country. Starlings' droppings foul buildings and pavements, and their voracious appetite can strip fields of corn. On the other hand, they eat leatherjackets, wireworms and other garden and farm pests. An expert mimic, the starling imitates other bird-calls and songs, incorporating them into its own song, largely a jumble of squeaks and whistles. Hundreds of thousands of starlings are present in Britain all year, and in winter their numbers are swollen by millions more that arrive from the Continent to take advantage of our milder winter climate. Nevertheless, starlings have declined dramatically in Britain – by almost 70 per cent in the past 35 years.

Juveniles mouse-brown, gradually becoming blackish with white spots, giving patchy appearance

Starlings often make nests in old woodpecker holes but any hole in a tree or cliff – or in houses and other buildings, including in cities – will do. Males begin making a nest before pairing.

Starling

Sturnus vulgaris

22cm

| J | F | M | A | M | J |
| J | A | S | O | N | D |

Found throughout Britain and Ireland apart from high mountains in many open habitats. Feeds mainly on grassland, from farm fields and parks to garden lawns, also on shores, rubbish dumps, town centres.

Adult in winter plumage heavily speckled with white

Feeds by inserting bill and opening it below ground while looking down and spotting insect larvae food

Sharply pointed yellow bill, with bluish base to lower mandible in breeding season

Starlings often hawk for flying insects in midair

After breeding, starlings often gather in huge flocks, performing amazingly co-ordinated aerobatic manoeuvres and calling noisily before settling to roost

GARDEN WATCHING

Declining but still familiar, starlings visit gardens all year round: in summer, one will sing from the chimney pot or television aerial, in late summer groups descend on berried bushes and to forage on the lawn, and in winter they come to bird tables.

Glossy, iridescent blackish plumage

Adult male in breeding season, with relatively few buff spots or none

Female has all-yellow bill. In both sexes, bill is dark grey in winter

Legs and feet are pinkish in spring, brown in winter

HOUSE SPARROW

AMONG THE MOST familiar of British birds, the house sparrow is, surprisingly, less numerous than the chaffinch, blackbird or wren. It is largely dependent on humans for its food and nesting places, but it is also likely to be due to humans that it has suffered the recent much publicised decline – likely factors include agricultural intensification and air pollution in urban areas caused by cars. A persistent 'chee-ip' is the commonest call, and the simple song a series of chirping notes. The sparrow's nest is a rather untidy affair in a hole or under the eaves of a building. Where there are no suitable man-made structures it will build a domed nest in a hedge, bush or tree.

Young birds beg for food from their parents by holding their bodies low and quivering their wings

Sparrows often dust-bathe in suitable spots on open ground in high summer, making small hollows in the dry earth

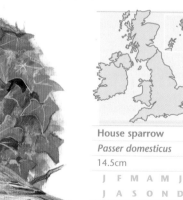

House sparrow

Passer domesticus

14.5cm

| J | F | M | A | M | J |
| J | A | S | O | N | D |

Towns, villages and farmland throughout Britain and Ireland, but recently in much reduced numbers.

Nests are often domed structures of straw and feathers when built in hedges; but in cities and towns an untidily lined hole in a building or tree will suffice

Grey crown and chestnut-brown area on rear of head

Large, untidy black bib

Male, breeding plumage

Dark-streaked chestnut-brown back

Pale grey cheeks and underparts

Female   Male

Female's plumage is far duller, without the grey crown or black bib

GARDEN WATCHING

Thick hedges, gaps in tiles or under eaves, and a supply of aphids in summer seem to be the necessary ingredients in a garden fit for sparrows. They especially like to gather together in noisy, squabbling groups inside a thick bush.

House sparrows mingle with finches in winter to feed on seeds

TREE SPARROW

THIS SLIGHTLY SMALLER and neater country cousin of the house sparrow is distinguished by a chestnut crown, white half-collar, neater bib and black cheek spot. Adults, both males and females, and young are all similarly marked. Populations fluctuate, and distribution is to some extent dependent on the availability of suitable nesting sites. In the 1970s and 1980s there was a massive decline of more than 80 per cent due to agricultural intensification. Breeding is in colonies; both sexes build the domed nest in a suitable hole or cavity in a tree, wall or cliff face or in a nest box, using dried grass or straw. In flight, tree sparrows give a high, distinctive 'teck-teck' call.

Courting birds bow and run at each other

GARDEN & PARK WATCHING

Gardens are rarely the place to spot tree sparrows. But they seem to like being close to water, so a town park with a lake might be a better bet, especially in summer, when there is a good supply of insects to feed on; in winter they need plenty of seeds.

Tree sparrow

Passer montanus

14cm

J F M A M J
J A S O N D

Far scarcer than house sparrows and less linked to humans. Lives mainly in open woodland, farmland with trees, orchards and quarries.

All-chestnut
crown

Black patch on cheek

Neat
black bib

Partial
white collar

GOLDFINCH

BLACK AND YELLOW wings flutter above a patch of thistles, teasels, groundsel or related plants in summer and early autumn as goldfinches cling to the seedheads of the plants and tweezer out and eat the seeds with their delicate bills. They use the thistledown, too, to line their neat nests in small trees or shrubs. The liquid, twittering song which once made the goldfinch a popular cage bird is heard as flocks, or 'charms', dance from plant to plant.

Young birds lack red and black head markings

Goldfinch

Carduelis carduelis

12cm

J F M A M J
J A S O N D

Farmlands, gardens and other open areas, except in mountains and moorland.

Black crown and
rear to head

Red
face

Black wings have
broad yellow bar

Sandy-brown body
and white belly

GARDEN WATCHING

In recent years goldfinches have taken to feed from hanging baskets and feeders with sunflower seeds and, especially, the much finer niger seed that sometimes acts as a magnet to these colourful finches.

CHAFFINCH

ONE OF THE British Isles' commonest birds – there are about 6 million pairs in Britain and over a million in Ireland – the chaffinch nests in hedges and trees. It feeds itself and its young on insects, but in winter roams widely in large flocks by day seeking seeds in fields and other open places. There is no mistaking the colouring of the male chaffinch when at rest, while in flight it shows its white shoulder patches and wing-bar. The nest is a cup of grass, moss and lichens, lined with hair. The loud cheerful, sweet rattling song starts slowly, accelerates down the scale and ends with an exuberant flourish; it is repeated up to five or ten times a minute. The alarm call is a loud 'pink, pink, pink'.

Chestnut back

White wing-bar and shoulder patch

Females less colourful but have same wing pattern

Chaffinch

Fringilla coelebs

15cm

J F M A M J
J A S O N D

Widespread, nesting in woods, scrub, hedges, parks and large gardens.

*Slate-blue
crown and neck
in summer*

*Wing pattern
visible when
perched*

*Pink-brown
below*

Male

*Male's bright
colours largely
obscured in winter*

GARDEN WATCHING

Older gardens
with fruit trees and
shrubberies are best
for chaffinches in
summer. In winter,
they come to bird
tables and often feed
on spilled seed
underneath; they are
not agile enough to
feed easily from a
hanging feeder.

BRAMBLING

THE BRAMBLING is a regular winter visitor and a few pairs have bred in Scotland in some recent years. But the male's splendid breeding plumage is a rare sight, as most birds leave to breed in northern Europe before attaining the full black head and back. In winter plumage, the male has buff mottling, greyish sides to the neck and a bright orange breast. Females are paler and lack the black on the head. Both sexes have a prominent white rump. The brambling's favourite food is beech mast – bramblings use their strong, sharp-edged bills to cut open the tough husks to get at the seed. The call note is a hoarse nasal, rising 'tsee-eep'.

Female duller, with dark areas mainly mottled brown

GARDEN WATCHING

This finch is very like a chaffinch in general shape, pattern and behaviour: it prefers feeding on the ground beneath a bird table when it comes to a garden, which it usually does in cold spells in winter.

Brambling

Fringilla montifringilla

14.5cm

J F M A M J J A S O N D

Widespread in winter, concentrated in woods and other areas with beech trees; sometimes in gardens, farmland and sewage works.

Bramblings often flock with other species in winter in search of seeds, especially beech

Bill yellow in winter

Orange-buff leading edge on wing

Glossy black head and beak in late spring

Orange-buff breast

Male in breeding plumage

Clear white belly

In winter, males resemble females but usually retain some black on head and back

GREENFINCH

BRIGHT YELLOW WING and tail flashes
help to identify the greenfinch against
a background of woodland and bushes.
It is a frequent visitor to town gardens,
especially when there is water for
bathing or peanuts on the bird table.
Greenfinches build their bulky cup
nests in bushes, using twigs, moss
or roots. The flight calls are a fast
twittering and hard 'jup jup jup', and
they have two different songs: one a
loud trill, often followed by a long,
wheezy 'djeeeee', the other a jumble
of trills, whistles and twitters rather
like that of a canary. In song flight
the male often flits and weaves
erratically with extra-slow wing-beats.

*Yellow wing and
tail flashes are
distinctive in flight*

GARDEN WATCHING

Tall hedges and
isolated ornamental
trees are good for
greenfinches in
summer. They are
also regular visitors
to berried shrubs such
as cotoneaster and
pyracantha, and to
hanging baskets of
seed and peanuts.

Greenfinch

Carduelis chloris

14.5cm

| J | F | M | A | M | J |
| J | A | S | O | N | D |

Widespread in
lowlands, in woods,
farmland with hedges,
gardens and other
areas with trees and
bushes; in winter also
on salt-marshes and
other open habitats.

Dark area
around eye

Brighter green
than female

Pink bill

Yellow on
wing and tail

Female duller, with
slightly streaked
underparts

Male

SISKIN

CONIFER FORESTS are the main home of the siskin, which feeds largely on the seeds of pine and spruce. It used to live only in the pine forests of the Scottish Highlands; though it now breeds more widely, most birds seen in southern Britain, including those on garden feeders, are winter visitors. Siskins like to flock together, often in alder trees during winter. Yellow-green in colouring, like the greenfinch, it is a distinctly smaller bird and the male has a black crown and chin. Siskins build their small, neat, cup-shaped nests high in conifer trees, and towards the tips of branches. The call is a loud, sharp 'tsing' or 'tsuu' and the song a mixture of twittering notes and long wheezy sounds.

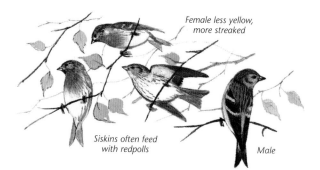

Female less yellow, more streaked

Siskins often feed with redpolls

Male

GARDEN WATCHING

Baskets of peanuts and niger seed bring siskins into gardens almost everywhere: sometimes, they return in successive years to the same feeder, but they may skip a year and return later. They are tiny, exquisite finches.

Siskin

Carduelis spinus

11.5cm

J F M A M J
J A S O N D

Breeds in coniferous forests, favours Norway spruce; and mixed woodland; in winter visits beech and alder trees, usually near water, and gardens for peanuts.

Black crown and chin

Yellow
wing-bars

Greenish-yellow
rump; yellow
tail-patches

Male

LINNET

IN VICTORIAN and Edwardian times linnets were often kept in cages for their musical song, a varied twittering heard between late March and late July. Now a protected bird, this small, slim finch faces a new enemy in the increased use of weedkillers, which are depleting the seeds of wild flowers such as chickweeds, fat-hen and dandelions which make up its diet. Linnets build their nests a few feet off the ground, often in gorse or bramble. The birds are a relatively rare sight in gardens.

Tail is quite long and forked

White edges to wing and tail feathers seen in flight

Male in spring

Female duller, more streaked

Linnet

Acanthis cannabina

13.5cm

J F M A M J
J A S O N D

Breeds mainly in open country with gorse and other dense bushes, farm-land with thick hedges, young conifer plantations and large gardens.

Grey head

Crimson
forehead

Crimson
patches on
either side of
breast in spring

Chestnut
back

GARDEN & PARK
WATCHING

This is not a common
garden bird but
occasionally nests in
low, thorny hedges
alongside large lawns;
it does not come to
feeders or bird tables.
In town parks, it can
be found in weedy
areas, feeding in flocks
on the ground.

LESSER REDPOLL

STREAKED BROWN with red and pink patches, like the linnet, the lesser redpoll's main distinguishing mark is its black chin. It nests in a variety of sites, from low gorse bushes and alder thickets to the high branches of silver birches and conifers. The nest is a cup of twigs, grass and plant stems. The redpoll's flight call is a rattling metallic trill. Flocks of redpolls often rise from the treetops and wheel in the air a few times before settling again.

Redpolls feed on tree and wild flower seeds

Lesser redpoll

Larger, paler common redpolls such as the bird on the right from northern Europe and Greenland may visit in winter

Common redpoll

Lesser redpoll

Acanthis cabaret

11.5-15cm

J F M A M J
J A S O N D

Widespread in woods, thickets, tall hedges and heaths with trees but has suffered an 80 per cent decline in the past 30 years.

In winter, redpolls feed in flocks on alder and birch seeds, often mixing with siskins

Red forehead. Dull red to yellowish on females

Neat black chin and black around base of bill

Small yellowish bill

GARDEN & PARK WATCHING

Look for this small finch in winter, often with siskins, in clumps of tall alders and birches beside the park lake. It is rare in gardens and rarer still at bird feeders. In summer it is much less widespread and harder to find.

Buff wing-bars

Red and pink breast and rump, brightest in spring – rarely seen on female

Forked tail

Male

BULLFINCH

DESPITE ITS BEAUTIFUL distinctive colouring, the bullfinch is not often seen; it is a secretive bird, generally keeping to cover in hedgerows and bushes. Often the only clue to its presence is the soft piping 'dew' of its call note. The male has bright, pinkish-red underparts, black cap, grey upperparts and a striking white rump. The female has a similar pattern, except for a duller, browner-grey back and dull salmon-pink underparts. Bullfinches often raid orchards to strip fruit trees of their young buds, the stubby bill being specially adapted for this diet. The birds breed mainly in woodlands with dense undergrowth but also in parks, thick hedges and scrubby areas, and large mature gardens. The nest of twigs, moss and lichens varies from a shallow platform to a bulky cup.

Juveniles (above right) are browner than females and lack the adults' black cap but do have the same white rump

Female

Female dull salmon-pink below

Bullfinch

Pyrrhula pyrrhula

15cm

J F M A M J
J A S O N D

Widespread except in extreme north and north-west; most numerous in southern England and southern Ireland.

Black cap; stubby bill

Male

White
wing-bar

White rump very
conspicuous
in flight

PInkish-red
underparts

Male

**GARDEN
WATCHING**

Sadly this dramatic
finch is declining
everywhere, but it is
a beautiful bird, worth
seeking out. It used
to be a garden pest,
eating fruit buds, but
numbers are now
mostly too low for this
to be an issue. Listen
for the low, simple,
whistled call.

HAWFINCH

Female

Female

Female plumage duller than male's with pale grey panel on wing

THE LARGEST OF BRITAIN'S finches also has the most powerful bill. It uses this to crack open the stones of fruit such as cherries and sloes to get at the edible kernels which form much of its diet. It also feeds on beech and hornbeam seeds, tree buds and insects. Hawfinches are very elusive birds, keeping mainly high up in the tree canopy in mature woodlands. An abrupt 'tik' occasionally indicates the bird's presence overhead. The nest, often built in an oak or fruit tree, is bulky, constructed of twigs and moss, and lined with roots and grass.

Big head, white-tipped short tail, broad white band on inner wing and white 'flash' on outer wing

Hawfinch

Coccothraustes coccothraustes

18cm

J F M A M J
J A S O N D

Mature deciduous and mixed woods, especially with hornbeam. Scattered distribution; most common in south-east England. Rare in Scotland and Wales; absent from Ireland.

Young bird lacks black bib and has dark bars on its belly

Large head

Pale grey nape

Massive, strong bill, blue-grey in breeding season, pale buff in winter

Chestnut body and head

GARDEN WATCHING

If you see this in your garden, you are especially favoured: it is a rare and secretive bird, but larger gardens, especially with cherries, hawthorns and hornbeams, may attract it. You may need to look early in the morning, as it is extremely flighty and easily disturbed.

Most visible in autumn and winter when they feed more on the ground

Male

REED BUNTING

ONCE CONFINED to reed-beds, marshes, fens and riversides, the reed bunting has spread to other, drier habitats. In summer the male's black head and throat are distinctive, and both sexes have a white moustache-like streak. Reed buntings often mingle with yellowhammers, house sparrows and finches in winter when they search for food. The song is a very simple, repetitive 'cheep-cheep-cheep-chizzup'. The nest, a cup of grass and moss lined with hair, is built on or close to the ground.

Brown head

Female

GARDEN WATCHING

In winter, a small, streaky bird with a long, black, white-sided tail may appear in the garden, even on a bird table: it might be a reed bunting, coming in from damper, waterside habitats to find an easy meal.

Reed bunting

Emberiza schoeniclus

15cm

| J | F | M | A | M | J |
| J | A | S | O | N | D |

Widespread near water in Britain and Ireland.

White 'moustache' joins white nape to form a broad collar

White collar on nape and outer tail feathers

Male

Black head and throat

Black streaked chestnut-brown upper parts

White outer tail feathers

Male, summer

YELLOWHAMMER

'A LITTLE BIT OF BREAD and no cheese' is a popular interpretation of the yellowhammer's song – a repeated series of notes ending in 'zeee' or 'chwee' – with some variations. The bird inhabits hedged fields, scrubby heathland and commons, feeding on seeds, berries, grain and insects. The male has a bright yellow head and breast, and a chestnut back streaked with black; its plain chestnut rump distinguishes it from the rare cirl bunting. Females are duller and more streaked. The nest is a neat cup of grasses.

Unstreaked chestnut rump

Streaked brown and black upper parts

Yellowhammer

Emberiza citrinella

16.5cm

J F M A M J
J A S O N D

Widespread in open areas with scrub or hedges; feeds on stubble and other fields in winter.

Bright yellow head

Male

Yellow breast

Incomplete dark-streaked chestnut band on breast

White tail outer feathers

PARK WATCHING

In the park, watch for yellowhammers in open spaces, on wire fences or on the tops of bushes. They like grassy areas in which to feed and a scattering of prominent perches. In summer, they sing all day long with their familiar, repetitive, metallic phrase.

BIRD WATCHING AND BEHAVIOUR

WELL STOCKED TABLE
A bird table with a shallow rim prevents food from being blown or washed away in bad weather. A large tray allows several birds to feed together.

Watching birds in your garden

MOST GARDEN BIRDWATCHING is best done from a window. If you have a deep enough window, pull up a comfortable chair and watch from there. Place bird feeders or a bird table high enough so that you can easily see them. A pond, or bird bath, is best put further from the house, for ease of viewing and so birds are less likely to be disturbed by your movements.

You can watch from a shed or even a purpose-built hide, but this is usually only useful if you want to photograph birds. If so,

you may need to place your viewpoint in the best position to take advantage of the sunlight, as well as creating some sort of narrow opening for your camera lens.

The physical birdwatching needs are simple, and you can attract many birds close to your house by feeding them (see pages 224-7). The rest is up to you: you can simply sit back and enjoy the birds as the mood takes you, or you can be more organised and undertake your own garden bird study.

HIGH RISE FEEDER
Modern bird feeders give a smooth, effective and efficient flow of seeds for several birds at a time with minimal competition and aggression. The use of plastic materials also allows for essential good hygiene.

SECRETIVE FISHERMAN *Grey herons are opportunistic enough to risk an early morning visit to a garden pond, in search of fish and frogs. They are easily disturbed, though.*

There are three groupings that you might look at in particular: nesting birds, feeding birds and resting, or roosting, birds. Nesting birds in gardens take something of a risk, but you can help them by reducing disturbance to a minimum once you suspect they are there. For example, try not to cut a hedge if birds are using it for nesting; and try to avoid long periods of potential disturbance, such as using a garden chair and table beside a shrub that has a nest inside it. Once you suspect the presence of a nest, it is easy enough to leave well alone for a couple of weeks. If birds are badly disturbed at a nest that contains eggs they may easily desert them. If they have chicks, they are less likely to desert them but they will need to get to and from the nest to feed them regularly and often. More of a problem are baby birds, such as those of a blackbird, which are prone to leap from the nest a few days too soon if you go too close. Don't be too tempted to 'take a peek'.

TWIGS AND TWINE
*Collared doves use thin
twigs, bits of string, even
lengths of wire, when
building their fragile nests in
trees, often in gardens or parks.*

Some birds nest in or on the fabric of your house: house sparrows and starlings and swifts, if you are lucky, in the roof; and house martins, outside, nesting up against the eaves. Swallows may nest in a garden shed. If you keep a note of these birds, and their nesting success, year on year, you can follow population trends.

Birds that are simply feeding in your garden are less of a worry. Many are scared from the lawn or the hedge many times a day, simply by your comings and goings in the garden, but this has little or no lasting effect. It helps, though, if you do not disturb feeding birds in cold weather.

You can study birds at a feeder, or feeding on the lawn, by keeping a daily or weekly checklist. Over the years, this can provide information of great use in bird surveys, especially if you keep records of the highest count each day for each species. Such studies form the basis of UK-wide garden bird surveys such as the annual Big Garden Birdwatch of the RSPB, in which more than 400,000 people may take part.

COSY IVY *House sparrows roost together in warm, sheltered places such as thickets of thorn or dense creepers, such as tangled ivy on walls.*

DOUBLE SHIFTS *Male blackbirds work hard when the female is incubating eggs, and then when there are young to feed. The female may lay a second clutch before the first chicks are independent.*

Roosting birds can be hard to spot – where some garden birds go at night is a bit of a mystery. But you may well hear the loud chorus of blackbird calls at dusk as they select the warmest, most sheltered and most secure roosting sites. Dense creepers against a house wall may attract groups of house sparrows to roost each evening. But there are many birds that use a house or garden simply as a resting place: collared doves, for example, will sit for long periods on top of a gable end, or on a TV aerial; woodpigeons and

crows may sit in a tall tree beside a garden, while having little to do with that garden.

Another category of birds are those that simply fly over a garden. These are not garden birds, but you can spot them from your lawn or a window. If you live close to water, even far inland, you may see passing gulls, cormorants, herons and perhaps common terns in summer. You might be on the regular route to and from a roost of rooks and jackdaws. Almost anything can turn up, so keep your eyes to the sky.

PROVIDING SEEDS *Allowing the right plants to grow – even weeds such as thistles – attracts birds that feed on their seeds and fruit, and on the insects they harbour.*

HYGIENE *Scrub bird-tables and clean feeders regularly – and clean out nest boxes after the breeding season is over. Always use cleaners that will not be harmful to the birds. It is also a good idea to move them about to avoid a build-up of waste below, which can lead to bacterial infection.*

WINTER BERRIES *Berry-bearing shrubs provide a rich source of food in winter when there is little else to eat. Blackbirds and other thrushes, finches, tits and starlings, feed on a variety of berries, including holly, rowan, barberry, hawthorn and cotoneaster. These plants may also attract migrants such as redwings, field-fares and, if you are lucky, waxwings.*

Making a safe haven for birds

ATTRACTING BIRDS TO YOUR GARDEN gives you great rewards. In return, you need to do the best for those birds, helping them to thrive in sometimes harsh modern conditions. There is usually nothing difficult about this, but you should bear several factors in mind.

The food you offer birds should be healthy and nutritious. Avoid cheap, especially mouldy, peanuts, which are potentially infected with deadly aflatoxin fungus. This is invisible, but it can kill small birds in large numbers. You should try to avoid peanuts and use sunflower seeds and other seed mixes instead. Also steer clear of cheap mixes with added biscuit (usually pale pink, green or yellow dog biscuit). If you do put out peanuts avoid spring and summer when birds are feeding young, unless you use a feeder with a small enough mesh to prevent the removal of whole nuts. Small birds may try to feed peanuts to chicks and choke them.

When you feed birds, keep the feeders and bird tables clean: occasionally wash them with

BIRD-TABLE FARE *Most kitchen scraps are suitable food for birds. Meat bones and fat are always popular, as are stale biscuits, cake, bread and cheese. Thrushes are very partial to fruit, however rotten, and many birds will eat boiled rice, potatoes and suet.*

PUTTING OUT FOOD *Tits feed from a fresh, halved coconut – but desiccated coconut should be avoided.*

WATER IS VITAL *Even in the coldest weather birds continue to bathe, for it helps them to keep their feathers in prime condition; and they always need water to drink. So an all-year-round supply of water is just as important as a regular source of food.*

a dilute disinfectant solution and brush away crusted droppings and other mess. Be careful to not to breathe in the dust and use separate bowls, brushes and washing-up gloves for this job. Accumulated bird droppings can spark off disease in birds in and around the garden, so move the feeders and tables from time to time, to reduce such harmful concentrations.

Watch for birds with swollen necks, open bills and breathing difficulties, or with canker affecting their feet and beaks which may have a rough encrustation. If you do see such problems, call a local vet or the RSPB for advice.

Use well-made feeding devices and avoid old-fashioned plastic mesh bags, or feeders based on a coiled spring design, which can trap birds by their feet, beaks or tongues. Experiment with different kinds of feeder, including ground tables and mesh covers designed to help small birds that prefer feeding from the ground.

Squirrels taking food left for birds can be a problem. There are deterrents, but even the best

NESTING BOXES *Many of the trees and shrubs which provide food for birds also offer places to nest. Few gardens are wild enough to offer many natural nest sites, so compensate for this by putting up nest boxes.*

FOILING THE CAT *Cats catch birds, but the damage can be reduced by using a bell or sonic deterrent on a safe, quick-release collar.*

are not foolproof. Loose-fitting baffles, rather like lampshades, beneath feeders on poles or above them on hanging wires, work well, but can look unsightly. You need to decide how much you can put up with squirrels, and whether you really need to prevent them from feeding.

The same applies to larger birds such as pigeons. Various designs of barrier (usually metal meshes) can keep out larger birds, as well as protecting smaller ones from sparrowhawks. You can also deter sparrowhawks with canes placed around a feeder, or even by hanging up reflective CD discs. Remember, though, that these deterrents risk damage to the hawks, who can be reckless in pursuit of prey, and may collide with such obstructions.

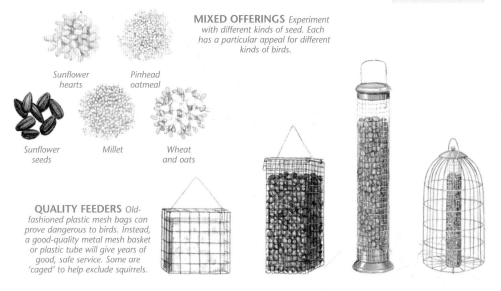

MIXED OFFERINGS *Experiment with different kinds of seed. Each has a particular appeal for different kinds of birds.*

Sunflower hearts

Pinhead oatmeal

Sunflower seeds

Millet

Wheat and oats

QUALITY FEEDERS *Old-fashioned plastic mesh bags can prove dangerous to birds. Instead, a good-quality metal mesh basket or plastic tube will give years of good, safe service. Some are 'caged' to help exclude squirrels.*

Cats can be a real problem. Domestic cats – and there are several million of them in the UK – each kill a few birds a year, which amounts to a toll of many millions. Some may kill one or two every week. Placing feeders away from bushes in which cats may lie in wait can help to reduce the number of birds killed. Otherwise, electrically operated, sonic cat deterrents (which emit harmless high-pitched sounds to scare cats away) may be the best solution, unless an owner fits a bell or a sonic device on a cat's collar. This,

done properly, with quick-release collars, can be effective without risking harm to the cat.

Birds also have a habit of flying into windows, thinking that a reflection is a real open space, sometimes with fatal results. You can help by using net curtains or sticking plastic shapes (often sold as bird shapes, but any will do) onto the glass to show that a hard surface is there. Accidents will happen, but with a bit of thought a garden can be made a safer place for birds, so adding to your enjoyment of them.

MIXED FLOCKS *Mixed finch, sparrow and bunting flocks used to be common on weedy farmland; now the land is too 'clean' for many seeds to be produced, and garden feeding can be a lifeline for such birds.*

Gardens as a refuge for farmland birds

A FEW DECADES AGO, after the harvest, fields would be left fallow to become overgrown with weeds. Wheat and barley were cut and the stubble was left until a new crop was sown in spring. Winter flocks of finches, buntings and sparrows in their hundreds would then swarm in these fields throughout winter.

Now, cereal fields are almost all sown in autumn, and by the following spring there is already a dense crop several inches tall. With improved herbicides, the crop is almost devoid of weeds. Such changes have huge implications for small farmland birds that eat insects in summer and seeds in winter. The supply of seed has been removed from the fields, the insects are much reduced, and so the finch and sparrow flock is almost a thing of the past. Ground-nesting birds such as skylarks find crops growing in spring too tall and thick.

Farmland, once a friendly habitat for country birds, has become a harsh environment. Many species, from skylarks, yellowhammers and tree

SEED BONANZA *Sunflower seeds in a feeder attract greenfinches – good for the garden bird-watcher and ideal for boosting the greenfinches' food intake in times of scarce natural foods.*

CATERPILLAR HARVEST *Even thick-billed finches such as the chaffinch need high-protein green caterpillars to feed to their growing chicks. Without them, their young will starve or become weak and vulnerable.*

sparrows to lapwings and grey partridges, have declined – so has the swallow, deprived of large flying insects. Caterpillars, another staple food, have also been hit, as the loss of food plants and the use of insecticides deplete moth numbers.

Gardens cannot help all these birds – skylarks and corn buntings, for example, will probably never be garden birds. But you can provide extra food and nesting places for some of them – even familiar ones such as starlings and house sparrows. Summer food, especially high-protein

insect food, essential for the healthy growth of chicks, is difficult to offer, but you can easily put out seeds for extra winter feeding.

You can help house sparrows, many of which have disappeared because of a lack of small insects, by avoiding garden pesticides, or reducing their use to an absolute minimum. Also, you can plant flowers and shrubs that attract insects: the RSPB can advise on what to plant to help harmless insects to thrive, as well as providing seeds and berries for birds.

DUNNOCK *A cheerful, high-pitched hurried-sounding series of broken warbling phrases comes from the dunnock. It likes to sing from the protection of a hedge or shrub.*

MISTLE THRUSH *A bird in full song during rain is likely to be the mistle thrush, also known as the storm cock. Its low song is wilder than a blackbird's, with broken phrases consisting of three to six short notes followed by a pause.*

WILLOW WARBLER *Although this is not a common garden bird, you may hear its sweet, musical phrase repeated at irregular intervals in spring and early summer.*

WREN *The wren utters 'tic tic' alarm calls and a remarkably loud, explosive song of clear, high-pitched warbling notes mixed with (and usually ending on) intense, rattling trills.*

Garden songsters

EVEN IN THE DEPTH OF WINTER some birds sing in the garden: listen for the song thrush, blackbird and, of course, the robin, one of our symbols of Christmas-time. If there are tall trees nearby you may also hear the energetic repetitions of the mistle thrush. More likely the fast, slightly flat song of a dunnock will draw your attention.

By early spring, the joyful, strident song of the great tit is easily recognised, while the blue tit has a more subtle phrase; the chaffinch joins in with a musical, rattling phrase. The three-note song of the collared dove may seem a little monotonous, but it is a dominant part of many suburban dawn choruses and more varied and appealing than it is often given credit for.

SONG THRUSH *A variety of short phrases are repeated in a loud, clear voice, such as 'Did he do it?' 'Did he do it?' 'Philip, Philip, Philip' and 'quick, quick, quick'.*

STARLING *If you think you heard a lapwing, curlew or golden oriole in the city, you've probably just been duped by a starling. These familiar garden birds are excellent mimics.*

ROBIN *The cascade of liquid warbling, with shriller notes and changes in tempo, comes from the robin: in autumn and winter it has a more melancholy quality. It sings all year round, with both sexes singing at times. It also sings at night, especially beneath the light of street or car park lighting, or under a full moon, when it may be optimistically mistaken for a nightingale.*

GREAT TIT *This vociferous bird's commonest forms of song are a shrill, see-sawing 'tea-cher tea-cher', and a repeated cry of 'pee-too, pee-too'.*

HOUSE SPARROW *The usual call is a persistent 'chissup' or 'chee-ip', often given by several birds in chorus; the song is a more deliberate repetition of similar but stronger notes, low in quality but high in enthusiasm and volume.*

These birds are not just singing for the sake of it – they are all vying for mates and laying claim to a territory, ready for the hard work of the breeding season just around the corner. There are still unexplained aspects of bird song: why might a tiny goldcrest, needing to feed every minute of the short winter days to be able to survive the cold nights, spend time and energy singing on a frosty morning? Why is bird song so complex and, to our ears, so musical, when a series of simple squawks might do? This can be more easily answered – the more complex the song the greater the skill, experience and fitness of the singer: the 'best' song identifies the male who is most likely to rear healthy broods of chicks.

BREEDING COLOURS *A male house sparrow in winter (right) has fresh feathers with pale buff-brown tips. They give it a pale, drab appearance. In spring, the feather tips crumble away to reveal brighter, stronger colours beneath, so that the breeding season male (left) is more striking. Also in spring, the bill turns from pale brown to black.*

RITUAL OF THE CARESS
Mutual fear and aggression are reduced between these woodpigeons by caressing one another.

Courtship rituals

THE 'LANGUAGE' OF BIRD courtship involves song, plumage and display. A bird uses these to spell out a number of messages – where it has established a territory; when it wishes to pair up; its sex and species; where it has found a possible nest site; and when it is ready to mate.

Most courtship begins in spring, before nesting gets under way. At this time the male usually takes the initiative. Some birds have special plumages, although few garden birds have the elaborate ornamentation seen on the great crested grebes on large park lakes and flooded gravel pits. The red breast of a robin is particularly stimulating to other robins; the size of the black bib on a house sparrow is important in courtship ('biggest is best') as is

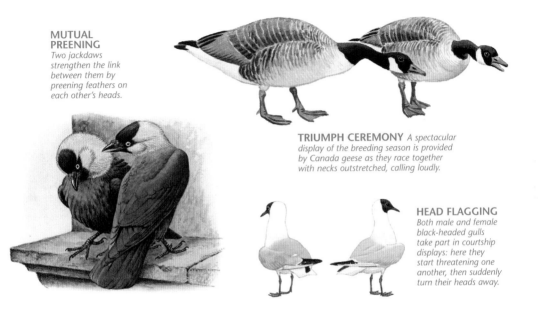

MUTUAL PREENING
Two jackdaws strengthen the link between them by preening feathers on each other's heads.

TRIUMPH CEREMONY *A spectacular display of the breeding season is provided by Canada geese as they race together with necks outstretched, calling loudly.*

HEAD FLAGGING
Both male and female black-headed gulls take part in courtship displays: here they start threatening one another, then suddenly turn their heads away.

the length of the tail streamers on a male swallow. Indeed, not only is length important, but so is symmetry, too: a swallow with one short or broken streamer is less likely to find a mate than a 'perfect' individual.

In species where male and female plumages are alike, birds are often aggressive to one another at first, until the pair sort out their appropriate responses and break down the barriers that normally maintain a physical separation between individuals. Building up a pair bond is essential if a pair are to come together to mate and then work as a partnership in rearing a family. They must invest a huge amount of time and energy, often at great risk to themselves, to breed successfully, and each

COURTSHIP FEEDING *Like a parent with a nestling, a male robin brings food in his bill and passes it on to the female, so helping to strengthen the bond between them.*

THE FEEDING RITUAL *Courtship feeding between hawfinches is at times totally ritualised, so that although their bills meet, no food passes between them.*

PRESENTING A FISH *A gift of food precedes copulation in kingfishers; the male presents a fish head-first to the female, so that she can swallow it without choking on the fins and scales.*

has to rely on the other: mutual trust and commitment are vital.

Once birds have become paired, the bond between them is strengthened by mutual preening, courtship feeding and picking out and showing a site where a nest might be built. This bond can be further strengthened by the joint defence of territory against rival birds.

Courtship feeding is more widespread than mutual preening. It is found chiefly in species in which the female carries out the duties of incubation alone. The form of the ritual varies, but generally the female behaves like a begging chick and the male feeds her as a parent would.

The courtship feeding of finches (see above) is usually extremely stylised in the early stages,

THE VITAL NEST SITE *Blue tits and other hole nesters investigate several nest holes. Exploration is usually initiated by the male, but the female makes the final choice.*

CHASE AND DISPLAY *A series of vigorous chases (below) starts when a female wren entices a male. Later, the male attracts the female to one of his nests by singing loudly, his tail and wings quivering.*

with male and female merely touching or 'scissoring' bills in a kind of kiss. As the breeding cycle progresses, the feeding tends to become more complete. In the bullfinch, for example, the male has often reached the stage of regurgitating food into his mate's bill by the time of nest-building, and this continues during the incubation period.

Displays designed to show the mate likely nest sites are especially well developed in birds which nest on the ground or (more likely in gardens) in holes in trees. The male great tit, for example, displays his black and white head pattern and the black and yellow of his underside, which show conspicuously against the dark entrance of a potential nest cavity.

WARBLER DISPLAY *The male garden warbler spreads his tail and flutters his wings in courtship display.*

COURTING A MATE *The male redstart begins his courtship by chasing the intended mate through the tree-tops. He shows off his red breast and black and white forehead, or, more usually, turns round and fans out his chestnut tail at the nest-hole.*

He then crouches, hissing before the female when ready for copulation.

Many species have special displays which indicate their willingness to copulate and which stimulate the partner to respond. Mating displays are not always by male birds only: there are often soliciting displays by females. The female blackbird points her bill and tail up almost vertically, sleeking her feathers and running a little in front of the male, giving a soft, high-pitched call. Although blackbirds are so common, their courtship displays are rather inconspicuous and often overlooked.

Most birds, including all typical garden birds, have no obvious external reproductive organs, merely a simple opening, called a cloaca, in both sexes. Although courtship can be so complicated and ritualised, copulation is usually a short,

HERON GREETING
Once the female heron is accepted at the nest site, the male starts flying out and returning with twigs. This leads to mutual 'greeting displays' each time he alights.

POSING MALLARDS
Like other ducks, male mallards have distinctive, ritualised courtship display postures.

simple affair, often a momentary bringing together of the cloacae (the male spreads his tail and swings the rear of his body downwards and sideways to effect the union). In some birds, though, it is repeated many times a day, far more than may be required to fertilise the eggs: this is partly to maintain and strengthen the pair bond, but also part of the male's desire to ensure that all his energies in rearing the resultant chicks will be devoted to furthering his own genes, not those of another male. Nevertheless, in most birds, many chicks are fathered by 'opportunistic' males that mate with promiscuous females. This may give the female a better chance to have the best father for her own offspring.

BLACKBIRD'S CUP NEST *After establishing a foundation by lodging material in a bush, hedge or tree, the female blackbird builds a strong, secure nest of grass, roots, moss and twigs plastered on the inside with mud and lined with fine grass. Blackbirds often use the same nest two or three times in a season, relining it each time.*

GOLDCREST'S HANGING NEST *Male and female goldcrests weave an intricate deep, cup-shaped nest of moss and spiders' webs, suspend it from a conifer branch and line it with feathers. The pair may construct a second nest in which the female lays her eggs before the first brood have left their nest; in this case the male feeds the first family.*

SWALLOW'S BRACKET NEST *A nail on a barn wall can provide all the support a swallow needs for its snug nest. Both sexes share the building, catching small straws and grass stems in the air and picking up mud with which to work them into pellets. The nest takes shape as pellets, placed on top of one another, harden.*

Nests and their builders

A NEST IS A SHELTER in a bird's battle for survival – a cradle in which eggs and helpless nestlings can be relatively safe from their enemies. The nest-building instinct is not found in all birds – cuckoos, for example, manage well enough without it.

There are two main types of nest – simple nests made by birds whose chicks are able to quit the nest and run on the day of hatching; and intricate nests of birds whose nestlings are born naked and helpless – and there are various stages in between. The simplest 'nest' is merely a depression in the ground or even a bare ledge on a cliff, but garden birds all make a more structured nest in a hole, bush or tree, or on a building – or inside it. Several species, including

CAMOUFLAGE *Well hidden under overhanging vegetation in holes in banks, robins' nests are all but invisible from a short distance.*

GREAT CRESTED GREBE'S NEST *Birds which nest on water may need substantial nests, but the nest construction is still basically simple – as with the great crested grebe's floating platform of water-weeds, reeds and rushes, anchored to the adjacent vegetation. When a grebe leaves the nest, it usually covers its eggs with weed as a defence against predators, though there is not always time.*

blue and great tits, starlings and house sparrows, nest in holes where their helpless young are well protected. There is often rivalry for sites among hole-nesters, and the same cavity may be used in successive years or even in the same season by different species. Song thrushes build cosy cup nests. Magpies protect their cup with a canopy of twigs. Wrens, willow warblers, wood warblers and chiffchaffs build more intricate domes, but none can vie with the long-tailed tit's beautifully made 'bottle' of lichen-covered moss, with the entrance hole placed near the top. House sparrows, starlings and jackdaws often nest on man-made sites; many birds will use nest-boxes, and robins, among other species, may even rear their broods in abandoned cars or vans.

INSECT EATERS

SWIFT *The swift has a huge gape to trawl for small, flying insects.*

WHITETHROAT *The whitethroat has a thin, forceps-like bill.*

TREECREEPER *This bird uses its long, slim down-curved beak to probe the tree bark.*

Bills and feeding techniques

ALTHOUGH BIRDS' BILLS vary greatly with feeding habits, even an unspecialised bill – like that of the song thrush – can be used to pick a minute gall-wasp from a leaf; to dig a 5cm hole to reach a beetle pupa; to tug an earthworm from the ground; to swing a snail shell against a stone; or to gulp down a ripe cherry. Gulls and crows, nature's scavengers, take a relatively wide range of both animal and vegetable foods with their all-purpose bills. Other birds are specialised feeders and depend on a fairly narrow selection of foods. This helps them to avoid competition within their preferred habitat. The kingfisher and the heron, for example, feed by seizing or spearing fish, and both have evolved dagger-shaped bills. Grey herons stalk through the

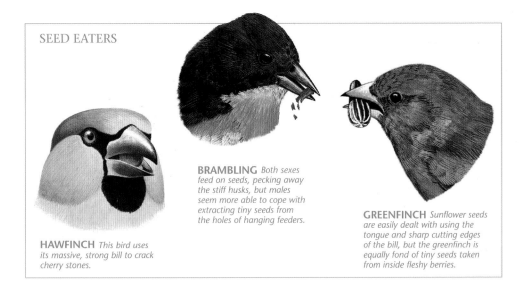

SEED EATERS

HAWFINCH *This bird uses its massive, strong bill to crack cherry stones.*

BRAMBLING *Both sexes feed on seeds, pecking away the stiff husks, but males seem more able to cope with extracting tiny seeds from the holes of hanging feeders.*

GREENFINCH *Sunflower seeds are easily dealt with using the tongue and sharp cutting edges of the bill, but the greenfinch is equally fond of tiny seeds taken from inside fleshy berries.*

shadows, seeking prey which they seize or stab with long bills. Kingfishers catch their prey with a shallow dive from a perch, then batter the heads of the fish on the perch, killing them and making them easier to swallow.

Owls catch prey by sight at dawn and dusk, or by sound after dark – they cannot see in the dark, but they can detect and pinpoint minute sounds. They are the night time predators that take over from the hawks and falcons that hunt by day, using sharp sight combined with speed and agility. The kestrel hovers to watch for food, while the sparrowhawk sits in wait ready to ambush prey, or dashes in to take small birds by surprise, using its short wings and long, broad tail to give maximum agility in the chase.

SHEARING *Mallards crop short grass and snip off shoots and underwater vegetation with their strong, broad bills.*

PROBING
Woodcocks use their long, thin bills, which have very sensitive tips, to probe for worms in soft earth.

SEIZING PREY
The grey heron's long, dagger-like bill is well suited to grabbing fish.

Nuthatches and great spotted woodpeckers wedge nuts in cracks of trees before splitting open the shells. Herring gulls get at the succulent flesh of mussels by dropping them from the air to shatter on the rocks below.

The rook, which eats many soil-dwelling insect larvae and earthworms, has a longer bill than that of its nearest relative, the carrion crow, which takes such food less often. Other soft-ground feeders, such as the woodcock and snipe, probe in soft mud. Each species avoids competition with others by probing at a different depth or in slightly different conditions. Male and female sparrowhawks avoid competition by being different sizes and eating different prey species.

TEARING *The hooked beaks of sparrowhawks and other birds of prey help to pluck the prey and tear off strips of flesh.*

HAMMERING *A green woodpecker chisels into bark for hidden insects with its powerful bill.*

BEATING *After making a capture, the kingfisher beats the fish's head against the branch.*

All finches have the strong conical bills typical of seed eaters; but each species has a slightly different bill. The most powerful, that of a hawfinch, can crack a cherry stone. At the other extreme, the far thinner billed goldfinch tweezers the seeds from teasels by probing.

Most birds drink when they can, though some species survive on 'metabolic' water – water released in the digestion of food. Crows bring water to their young by transporting it in the throat. All birds conserve water by producing a very highly concentrated urine – which is almost a paste of uric acid crystals. In very dry weather they reduce the time and effort spent singing and, with it, evaporation of moisture from the lungs.

PREENING *A male blackbird 'zips up' his wing feather barbs; his mate nibbles her undertail feathers. Preening removes feather parasites – a vital operation; birds that are ill or have malformed or damaged bills, preventing adequate preening, often have an abnormally large number of parasites which eat away the feathers and affect general health.*

INDIRECT SCRATCHING *A chaffinch scratches its head by drooping a wing, then bringing its foot up over its shoulder. The majority of British songbirds and birds of some other groups, such as swifts, nightjars and kingfishers (but not woodpeckers) scratch indirectly.*

DIRECT SCRATCHING *With wings closed, a lesser black-backed gull reaches a leg forward to scratch its head feathers.*

Plumage – keeping feathers clean

FEATHERS ARE NOT INDESTRUCTIBLE and careful maintenance is vital to a bird's well-being.
PREENING This habit, shared by all birds, is the treatment of feathers by the bill. With body feathers fluffed up, a bird 'nibbles' individual feathers between the tips of its bill, working from the base of the quill outwards, with a series of precise pecking movements. The bird also draws feathers – particularly those of wings and tail – one at a time through its bill, with a single, quick pull of the head. This cleans the plumage, works in oil from the preen gland just above the tail, puts feathers back in place and repairs vanes and webs by 'zipping up' the tiny barbs.
SCRATCHING A bird cannot preen its own head, so it scratches with one foot while balancing on

BATHING *Fluffing up its body feathers, a song thrush hops into the water and first dips forward with head, breast and wing-joints in the water, at the same time shaking its bill violently from side to side and flicking its wings forward. Then it squats back, with tail and belly in the water, and flicks its wings upwards to send the water splashing and showering.*

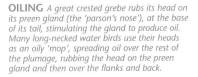

OILING *A great crested grebe rubs its head on its preen gland (the 'parson's nose'), at the base of its tail, stimulating the gland to produce oil. Many long-necked water birds use their heads as an oily 'mop', spreading oil over the rest of the plumage, rubbing the head on the preen gland and then over the flanks and back.*

the other. A few, such as gannets and herons, have a pectinated claw – a special 'comb' on the inside edge of the third toe – used to scratch the head and neck. Some paired birds, including crows, bearded tits, martins and pigeons, preen one another's heads as part of courtship.

BATHING Apart from cleansing, the main object of bathing for many birds is to dampen the plumage so that preen oil may be spread over it more effectively. Land birds bathe in shallow water where they can stand safely – puddles, the edges of streams or ponds and bird baths. Water birds spend more time over bathing because they are usually safe on open water. After bathing, birds shake their feathers and flap their wings to dry themselves. Cormorants on

DUSTING *House sparrows make scrapes in the ground, then work dust into their feathers. Other birds, including gamebirds, owls, hoopoes, certain hawks and nightjars, wrens and skylarks, also enjoy dust baths. The habit probably helps to combat feather parasites.*

SUNNING *A blackbird spreads its wings and tail in the sunshine – possibly as an aid to keeping down the numbers of feather parasites. It may also be a cooling device, helping the bird to lose heat through exposing sparsely feathered areas to the air and breeze.*

the park lake will perch on a buoy or post and 'hang out' their wings to dry.

OILING After its bath, the bird oils its plumage, applying a secretion from its preen gland. Oiling waterproofs plumage and maintains its heat-insulating properties; it is particularly important to water birds and very small land birds.

SUNNING Birds sun themselves by lying out in the sun with tail and one or both wings spread. It is thought that this may help to make parasites move about so the bird can pick them off more easily; and that the sun's ultra-violet light may convert the preen oil into vitamin A, which can be ingested when the bird preens.

POWDERING Some birds, such as gamebirds, do not bathe in water; and others, including some

INDIRECT ANTING *A jay allows worker ants to run all over its plumage, deliberately arousing them so that they aggressively squirt out their formic acid. The jay leans back on its tail, with wings spread out in front of it; the blackbird, song thrush and mistle thrush half squat among the ants with wings out; and the carrion crow and rook lie down, spread-eagled, to wallow among the ants.*

DIRECT ANTING *The starling gathers a billful of ants and rubs them on its flight feathers, spreading formic acid and any other body fluids of the ants, together with its own saliva. Chaffinches and meadow pipits use a single ant at a time.*

pigeons, do not oil. Instead they powder themselves using powder-down – modified body feathers that grow continuously and disintegrate into a fine 'talc' of tiny, dusty particles that permeate the plumage when the birds preen.
DUSTING Gamebirds, such as pheasants and grouse, dust themselves in dry, fine earth, grit or sand. They scrape hollows in the ground and work the dust up among the feathers, shaking it all out before preening.
ANTING In this bizarre habit, birds use formic-acid-producing worker ants. Birds may ant for the sensuous pleasure of having their skins stimulated by formic acid – but it has a practical purpose: formic acid is an insecticide strong enough to kill feather mites.

FLOWER PECKERS *House sparrows habitually peck yellow flowers, especially crocuses. No one really knows why they do it.*

CHICK THIEVES *Magpies eat small bird chicks when they can find them; but the following year, the same small birds are likely to nest in the same place again. The magpie's behaviour can be upsetting, but it rarely has any lasting effect on songbird numbers.*

Delinquent birds

NATURE CAN BE BEAUTIFUL but is not always nice. Every creature has to eat, and most birds are omnivorous or carnivorous to a degree. Blackbirds eat worms; blue tits eat caterpillars; spotted flycatchers take butterflies. People may be horrified at a sparrowhawk killing a dove on the lawn, but love the 'wise owl' asleep in the ivy, forgetting that tawny owls kill many small birds, too. They just do so at night.

You may have cause to curse some birds. Sparrows rip apart yellow crocuses in spring.

Blackbirds eat red and black currants. Bigger birds, such as woodpigeons, may create havoc in the fruit and vegetable garden. Pigeons, including collared doves, leave thick, messy droppings. Blackbirds scatter soil from patio pots as they search for worms. Blue tits tear wallpaper and peck at putty in spring.

The real debates, though, are sparked by the bigger predators. Sparrowhawks prey on small birds, but if they wiped them out, they would starve. Predator and small bird have lived

HAWK ATTACK *Feeders and bird tables concentrate small birds in perfect 'feeding stations' for sparrowhawks. It is an unavoidable risk when helping birds this way.*

PUTTY PICKERS *Blue and great tits often pick at putty around windows, sometimes seeming to become addicted to this behaviour for no obvious reason. It seems to be a natural habit of exploring for food taken to excess.*

together for millions of years: the presence of hawks means there must be plenty of prey.

Urban magpies are encouraged by our waste food, and the number of animals killed on our roads. So we get what we deserve. In spring, magpies can turn to the eggs and chicks of small birds. Their effect on overall numbers is minimal, but locally – in the context of a few gardens – they can seemingly devastate small bird populations. It is undeniably distressing to see a magpie killing a fledgling, but this is the way that nature operates and, in the end, we have to learn to live with it.

Where there is plenty of food, there will be something to eat it, as a rule. Killing magpies, for example, in an area of suburban gardens, would have little effect: more magpies would simply move in to take the place of those that have been removed. It is better to provide safer places for birds to nest than to try to remove all their potential predators, which are, after all, simply doing what they have evolved to do.

ELEGANT VISITORS
Spotted flycatchers arrive from Africa in late spring or early summer, and often nest in gardens, churchyards and parks. They are, though, declining, for reasons that are still obscure but probably centre around lack of insect food and difficult conditions in their wintering areas.

Residents versus migrants

MOST GARDEN BIRDS have short lives. The blackbird that has been coming to feed for ten years is usually a succession of blackbirds, all of which look much alike, taking advantage of good feeding conditions. But there are birds that can be seen all year round in a garden, and others that return year after year to the same place, even though they journey huge distances.

The blackbird may be a resident or a migrant; many gardens have both. After nesting, a pair of blackbirds usually split the brood between them and take them to the countryside. They return later in the year and may remain until the following spring. From late autumn to spring, other blackbirds in the garden may have come from mainland Europe to enjoy Britain's milder winter weather. Similarly, starlings in winter may include many from the Continent that migrate back over the sea in spring.

Swallows return to nest year after year in the same spot and, if both survive, pair with each other once again: their young nest a few miles

HIGH FIDELITY *Many small birds such as willow warblers and swallows return to the same territory year after year. Their offspring tend to move away a short distance, preventing inbreeding.*

NEW WINTER BIRD *Blackcaps were not often recorded in winter in Britain until a few decades ago. Now several hundred spend each winter here, scattered widely from Scotland to the south of England.*

away, a natural barrier against inbreeding. Willow warblers, which fly to Africa each winter, sing from the very same tree in successive springs – they even feed in the same bushes in successive years in Africa, too.

Blackcaps nest in summer in Britain and leave in autumn, but some German blackcaps spend the winter here. So, the blackcap you see in summer will not be the same one that comes to the bird table in January. Siskins often appear at bird feeders in late winter and spring when

natural food is scarce. Some will come back the following year; others may spend the next winter in a different part of Europe, though even these may come back to the garden a year later, depending on the availability of natural foods.

Even groups of blue tits that seem to favour a particular garden are incurable wanderers. If you have a dozen blue tits on the feeder all day, you might see 50 or even 100 different ones over a few days, as roaming flocks cover the local woods and suburbs in long, irregular circuits.

INDEX

Page numbers in bold type
refer to the main entry.

Wild Britain: Garden Birds is based on material in *Reader's Digest Guide to Britain's Wildlife, Plants & Flowers; Nature Lover's Library: Field Guide to the Birds of Britain* and *Book of British Birds* published by The Reader's Digest Association Limited, London.

Origination by Colour Systems Limited, London
Printed in China

We are committed both to the quality of our products and the service we provide to our customers. We value your comments, so please do contact us on **08705 113366** or via our website at
www.readersdigest.co.uk

If you have any comments or suggestions about the content of our books, email us at
gbeditorial@readersdigest.co.uk

Book code 400-374 UP0000-1
ISBN 978 0 276 44271 1
Oracle code 250011835H.00.24

Acknowledgments

COVER f and **b** NHPA/Laurie Campbell; 2-3 ShutterStock, Inc/Ian Edward Schofield; 22-23 naturepl.com/Kim Taylor; 219-20 naturepl.com/Andrew Parkinson
MAPS Jennie Doodge
ILLUSTRATIONS Stephen Adams; Norman Arlott; Norman G. Barber; Peter Barrett; Trevor Boyer; Kathleen Flack, John Francis ; Eric Fraser, Robert Gillmor; Tim Hayward; Hermann Heinzel; Mick Loates; Robert Morton; Philip North Taylor; D.W. Ovenden; Rosemary Parslow; Ken Wood Pages; Sydney Woods

EDITORS John Andrews, Lisa Thomas
ART EDITOR Austin Taylor
EDITORIAL CONSULTANT Rob Hume
PROOFREADER Ron Pankhurst
INDEXER Marie Lorimer

Reader's Digest General Books
EDITORIAL DIRECTOR Julian Browne
ART DIRECTOR Anne-Marie Bulat
MANAGING EDITOR Nina Hathway
HEAD OF BOOK DEVELOPMENT Sarah Bloxham
PICTURE RESOURCE MANAGER
Sarah Stewart-Richardson
PRE-PRESS ACCOUNT MANAGER Dean Russell
PRODUCTION CONTROLLER
Katherine Bunn
PRODUCT PRODUCTION MANAGER
Claudette Bramble